REAL MARKETS: SOCIAL AND POLITICAL ISSUES OF FOOD POLICY REFORM

The United Nations Research Institute for Social Development (UNRISD) was established to promote in-depth research into the social dimensions of pressing problems and issues of contemporary relevance affecting development. Its work is inspired by the conviction that, for effective development policies to be formulated, an understanding of the social and political context is crucial, as is an accurate assessment of how such policies affect different social groups. The Institute attempts to complement the work done by other United Nations agencies and its current research themes include the social impact of the economic crisis and adjustment policies; environment, sustainable development and social change; ethnic conflict and development; political violence and social movements; refugees, returnees and local society; the socio-economic and political consequences of the international trade in illicit drugs; patterns of consumption; qualitative indicators of development; and participation and changes in property relations in communist and post-communist societies.

Real Markets: Social and Political Issues of Food Policy Reform

edited by
CYNTHIA HEWITT DE ALCÁNTARA

FRANK CASS • LONDON

in association with
The European Association of Development Research
and Training Institutes (EADI), Geneva
and
The United Nations Research
Institute for Social Development
(UNRISD), Geneva

First Published 1993 in Great Britain by
FRANK CASS AND COMPANY LIMITED
Gainsborough House, 11 Gainsborough Road,
London E11 1RS, England

and in the United States of America by
FRANK CASS
c/o Internatinal Specialized Book Services, Inc.,
5804 N.E. Hassalo Street, Portland, Oregon 97213-3644

British Library Cataloguing in Publication Data

Real Markets: Social and Political Issues
of Food Policy Reform. – (Special Issue
of "European Journal of Development
Research", ISSN 0957-8811;Vol.4, No.2)
   I. Alcantara, Cynthia Hewitt De
   II. Series
   338.1

   ISBN 0-7146-4514 1

Library of Congress Cataloging-in-Publication Data

Real markets : social and political issues of food policy reform /
edited by Cynthia Hewitt de Alcántara.
   p. cm.
   "This group of studies first appeared in a special issue on 'Real
markets: social and political issues of food policy reform' of the
European journal of development research, v. 4, no. 2, December
1992, published by Frank Cass & Co. Ltd."—T.p. verso.
   Papers presented at a Seminar on Food Pricing and Marketing
Reforms, sponsored by the United Nations Research Institute for
Social Development (UNRISD) and held in Geneva during November 1989.
   Includes bibliographical references.
   ISBN 0-7146-4514-1
   1. Produce trade—Developing countries—Congresses. 2. Nutrition
policy—Developing countries—Congresses. I. Hewitt de Alcántara,
Cynthia.
HD9018.D44R43   1993
363.8'09172'4—dc20   92-41261
                                                     CIP

This group of studies first appeared in a Special Issue on 'Real Markets: Social
and Political Issues of Food Policy Reform' of the *European Journal of
Development Research*, Vol. 4, No. 2, December 1992, published by Frank Cass
& Co Ltd

Printed by Antony Rowe Ltd, Chippenham, Wiltshire

Contents

Acknowledgements

Introduction: Markets in Principle
and Practice   **Cynthia Hewitt de Alcántara**   1

Paths of Authority: Roads, the State and the
Market in Eastern Zaire   **James Fairhead**   17

The Finance of Trade and Agriculture in   **Ben Crow and**
a Backward Area of Bangladesh   **K. A. S. Murshid**   36

Real Foodgrains Markets and State Intervention
in India   **Barbara Harriss**   61

Urban Bias Revisited: Staple Food Pricing in
Tanzania   **Deborah Fahy Bryceson**   82

The Political Economy of Food Pricing and
Marketing Reforms in Nicaragua, 1984–87   **Peter Utting**   107

Acknowledgements

Real Markets: Social and Political Issues of Food Policy Reform contains papers presented at a Seminar on Food Pricing and Marketing Reforms, sponsored by the United Nations Research Institute for Social Development (UNRISD) and held in Geneva during November 1989.

Financing for the seminar was provided by the Directorate-General for Development of the Commission of the European Communities.

The authors would like to thank other participants in the seminar for their thoughtful comments: Nick Amin, Kirsten Appendini, Sartaj Aziz, Nyangabyaki Bazaara, Solon Barraclough, Hubert Morsink, Johan Pottier, Philip Raikes, Hans-Otto Sano, Yassin Wehelie and Ann Zammit. They are also grateful to the Director of UNRISD, Dharam Ghai, and to two representatives of the European Commission, Walter Kennes and B. Amat, for supporting the conference; and they wish to express their appreciation to David Lehmann and Maureen Mackintosh for providing insight and encouragement during the preparation of the manuscript for publication.

Irene Ruiz de Budavari and Wendy Salvo contributed indispensable administrative assistance for the project, and Jenifer Freedman copy edited the following texts.

Introduction:
Markets in Principle and Practice

CYNTHIA HEWITT DE ALCÁNTARA

I

If development policy in the 1980s was consistently shaped by an appeal to market principle, rather narrowly defined, the process of reform in the 1990s already shows signs of increasing concern with market practice – with what a growing number of people are calling the political economy of 'real markets'.[1]

This is the case for a number of reasons. The first is simply the experience of the past decade, which has forcefully illustrated the complexity of efforts at economic restructuring around the world and the difficulties encountered when insufficient attention is paid to a wide range of real market settings in which reform programmes are being applied.

As a lending condition, international financial institutions have routinely imposed a standard set of policy prescriptions, intended to 'get prices right', on a large number of Third World countries with debt-related balance of payments difficulties. Although economic stabilization in a narrow sense has been attained with a certain frequency, this has very seldom led to renewed growth; and it almost always has had regressive effects on income distribution and general welfare [*Ghai, 1991; Taylor, 1988*]. Furthermore, in many cases, even stabilization itself has proved consistently elusive.

Particularly unsettling for observers of market reforms is the fact that one of the most prominent assertions made by proponents of these programmes, who hoped to better conditions in rural areas, has proved very unreliable in practice. It was consistently predicted that the standard set of corrective measures lying at the centre of reform (including devaluation, reduction of trade barriers and curbs on the role of the state in agricultural marketing) would be strongly favourable to farmers, and in particular to small cultivators or peasants. 'Shifting the terms of trade toward agriculture' was a principal goal of the reform process, and this was expected to provide strong impetus for improving rural livelihood [*World Bank, 1981; 1986*].

After almost ten years of experience, however, there is abundant evidence that the standard package of market-oriented reforms required to pursue macroeconomic stabilization has not, on the whole, been of benefit to small farmers, and that most rural people are today worse off than they were before the policy experiment began.[2] This is not to say that they might not have suffered equally, or more, if nothing at all had been done to confront economic crisis. It is to say that such an outcome can be expected to raise legitimate questions concerning the adequacy of the set of assumptions utilised to devise a policy remedy.

The central assumption underlying the effort to deal with crisis in many Third World countries during the 1980s has been a relatively rigid one, based on a logical construct (the 'free market') which is open to theoretical and practical challenge on a number of grounds. In its most simplistic form, the assumption holds that resources are allocated in an optimally efficient manner through the impersonal play of supply and demand; and that the roots of crisis lie in the systematic 'distortion' of market signals through inappropriate government interference with free market forces. Since relative prices constitute the basic instrument of market regulation, removal of factors (like fixed exchange rates, price controls and subsidies, restrictions on imports, export taxes and so forth) impeding the automatic adjustment of these prices constitutes, in this view, the single most important step which can be taken to revive economies and – in largely agrarian societies – to ensure that rural people enjoy increased opportunities [*World Bank, 1981; 1986*].

Macroeconomists outside the neoliberal school have long criticised this form of 'free market' analysis for its reductionism: it posits mechanisms of adjustment on the basis of a deductive exploration of the logic of maximising, not on the basis of empirical investigation [*Robinson, 1977; Polanyi, 1957*] Economists have also pointed out repeatedly that relative prices do not shift in ways which promote greater welfare for greater numbers within a context of fundamentally unequal distribution of resources. In the absence of structural reform, the unfettered working of the market is no guarantee of development.

At a more practical level, development economists have consistently challenged the notion that price distortion constitutes the most important problem of the agricultural sector in most Third World countries, drawing attention instead to the problem of ensuring that small cultivators are provided with the kind of basic infrastructure and support services they require to gain any benefit from more advantageous prices [*Lipton, 1987; Pinstrup-Andersen, 1989*]. And a steady stream of country-level case studies has also convincingly illustrated the practical difficulties confronted by governments attempting to implement pricing and marketing reforms within a context of generalised economic crisis, deteriorating communications networks, foreign exchange shortage and concomitant restrictions on the importation of basic producers' goods [*Kydd, 1986; Harrigan, 1988; Ig-*

bedioh, 1990; Sahn and Arulpragasam, 1991; Commander, Ndoye and Oedrago, 1989]. 'Getting prices right' in one area of the economy (as through devaluation of the national currency, for example) can have potentially disastrous consequences for other areas, including agricultural production.

All of these criticisms suggest that if the economic crisis of the past few decades, and more specifically the livelihood crisis of rural areas, is to be tackled as adequately and creatively as possible, policy reform must be far more soundly grounded in a careful understanding of concrete local situations than it has usually been in the past. The more rigidly deductive elements in prevailing economic prescriptions must be tempered by further analysis of the complex processes of social and economic change which form the 'real world' of macroeconomic adjustment and restructuring.

The international funding agencies, in association with donor countries, have attempted to address this need by setting up programmes of survey research oriented toward documenting changes in welfare and socio-economic structure in a number of Third World countries [*Delaine, et al, 1992*]. Their effort is an important one, generating information which was previously unavailable. It will permit social scientists and policy-makers to monitor certain trends. It cannot, however, provide a substitute for the kind of qualitative research designed to analyse the structure and functioning of social institutions and to observe the concrete dynamics of social change in particular local settings.

One of the institutions most in need of study at present is, in fact, the market – not as it is hypothesised to function in neo-liberal economics, but as it is substantiated (to use Karl Polanyi's term) or made operative through the interaction of real social groups. Markets are culturally and politically specific institutions: the significant difference in the way they function, even within the relatively narrow field of highly developed capitalist economies, is surely a telling illustration of this basic point. Societies – even when formally lumped within the same taxonomic category – have different histories and values. The balance of power among major groups within each country is peculiar, and principal players adhere to historically specific rules of the political game. A varying degree of vulnerability to external forces (or capacity for external alliance) affects the capacity to manoeuvre in innumerable concrete cases. All of this makes for distinct allocative priorities and forms of regulation, and thus for qualitatively different 'real markets'.

It is precisely the enormous variation in 'real markets' which lies at the heart of what reform-minded advisors to Third World governments tend to categorise as problems of policy implementation. A standard policy package, designed in the abstract, cannot be implemented in the abstract. It will be warped and molded by social forces which are, in the last analysis, ideosyncratic. And in the passage through real markets, measures which in a given context might originally have been expected to favour one group may actually favour another; incentives designed to ensure a much-desired pattern of response may in fact inspire its opposite; and hypothesised patterns of reinforcement or interaction between elements in the package may prove, in the last analysis, to be highly problematic. In many cases, reform measures introduced at the national or regional level simply never reach the local level at all.

This statement is as applicable to reform efforts in socialist settings as in capitalist or semi-capitalist ones. Both 'transitions to socialism' and 'transitions from socialism' in developing countries have been plagued by the same kinds of problems afflicting stabilisation and adjustment efforts within the non-socialist Third World over the past few decades. A great many assumptions about the nature of existing markets have in practice proved illusory (most particularly when Third World governments have implemented socialist reforms in rural markets, insufficiently understood by urban-based planners) [*Mackintosh, 1986*; *Spoor, 1991*].

Similar problems arise in Eastern Europe and the ex-Soviet Union, now involved in an unprecedented experiment to create capitalist institutions. Reforms in these countries are often based upon an extremely stylised and formalistic vision of how market societies work; and it is obvious that some of the institutions and policies currently being imported will not be congruent with the existing social and cultural milieu or with any reasonably likely pattern of change within it. A broad-ranging debate within the international community on the complex world of 'real markets' might provide some counterweight to unrealistic expectations in this context.[3]

II

The articles included in this volume explore the interface between policy prescription, on the one hand, and real Third World food markets on the other.[4] Some essays are particularly concerned with local exchange environments, and others with the political economy of market reform. Taken together, they contribute elements for rethinking experiments in market reform, from the bottom up; and they illustrate why policy prescriptions are likely to have a variety of unintended consequences in different parts of the world.

The first point which emerges clearly in the following pages is simply that *a great many rural people around the globe are only tenuously integrated into wider markets of any kind.* Over centuries, the population of the Third World has been drawn into – and sometimes later expelled from – shifting markets for commodities and labour created by the commercial and political expansion of empires. Many remote communities, where contact with the outside world now seems extremely limited, have in fact participated at some earlier historical moment in once-dynamic markets, later eliminated by the vagaries of history.

Current isolation is therefore not likely to reflect a past in which there was no contact with wider forces. Truly 'primitive' groups are difficult to find in our day. But hundreds of millions of people are currently living on the fringes of markets, caught up in a very chaotic and contradictory process of incorporation into developing political and economic systems which make new demands on their allegiances and resources, and wreak havoc with their lives.[5]

In this context, the market is experienced differentially. As James Fairhead shows in the following chapter, it advances in conjunction with very complex political forces, creating opportunities for some and grave dangers to livelihood for others. It affects social relations throughout communities, kin groups and families; it changes the structure of rights and obligations for men and women within households. And the very incompleteness of market integration, whether for commodities or labour or land, implies the existence of extraordinarily varied survival strategies, altered with great frequency.

To think that steps introduced to 'get prices right' within the macroeconomy can have any straightforward effect on most people in situations like these is naive – just as it is naive to suppose that measures introduced in the past by the majority of Third World socialist governments to create state marketing structures could have been implemented coherently in such a context.

In cases like that described by Fairhead, most rural households continue to have access to land; and they pursue a subsistence strategy in which nonmonetary reciprocity still plays an important, though declining, part. They can exchange goods within and among families and clans without necessarily having to earn or spend money. Their livelihood, although circumscribed by dependence upon the protection and largesse of a chiefly hierarchy, is still to some degree under their own control.

Over large areas of the world, however, the survival of rural people depends on long-standing and rigid relations of subordination, whether within the context of feudal society or within a structure of mercantile power which stands between a local peasantry and the wider economic and political system. For example, the most densely populated country in Africa, Rwanda, contains regions in which the persistence of semi-feudal relations has seriously complicated the task of creating a viable national food market. There is great pressure on the land, controlled in the northern region by an elite which rents small parcels to its clientele, or allows the latter access to plots in return for the delivery of a part of the harvest and/or the provision of labour services.

Food markets in the semi-feudal setting of northern Rwanda are narrow and oligopolistic. In the recurring periods of drought and hunger which afflict the country, trading interests work not to move production from surplus to deficit regions but to channel basic foodstuffs toward areas where people are better off and effective demand highest. Such a situation constitutes a textbook example, explained by Amartya Sen [1981], of how market mechanisms can actually bring on famine in regions where grain could in fact be supplied but effective demand provides no incentive to do so. The government has therefore been repeatedly urged by international advisors and donors not to get out of marketing but to get into it, in order to regulate distribution; but there has been only modest response [Pottier, 1989].

Some of the most elaborately hierarchical structures of market exchange in the world are to be found on the Indian subcontinent, where private trade in backward regions is grounded in multiple mechanisms of coercion and control. An extreme example of an exploitative marketing system is analysed in the paper by Ben Crow and K.A.S. Murshid, who have studied the real world of paddy and rice trading in a relatively isolated rural area of Bangladesh. As in northern Rwanda, the power of the local elite in the Bangladeshi case rests on the control of land and credit, made available to poor peasants in return for a proportion of their output and/or the provision of labour services. Market dominance is further ensured by a transport cartel, by control over local political and judicial institutions and, when necessary, by the use of force.

Such a situation clearly illustrates the *inadvisability of assuming that private trade is necessarily synonymous with free markets*. On the contrary, private trade can be facilitated precisely by forcing peasant households into relations of dependence and indebtedness which lead to what Amit Bhaduri [1986] has called 'forced commerce': poor producers sell more than they should, to pay their debts, and then fill the gap in family subsistence by buying back basic foodstuffs at high prices later on in the year. The system operates within a framework of interlocked markets for land, labour, credit and commodities which is the antithesis of the 'free market' model.

Between the pole of incipient market integration, represented in these pages by the Zairian case, and that of complete integration under extremely exploitative conditions, described for Bangladesh, there are a great many intermediate situations, in which rural people have greater or lesser opportunities to participate in wider exchange environments under conditions enabling them to obtain a fair return for their goods or their labour. It is important to note that these conditions vary markedly not only among countries, but – more interestingly, perhaps, for policy prescription – within countries and even within provinces or states. The physical setting of certain regions, the crops they produce and the food they consume, their social and political history and current status within national development projects or struggles – all affect the 'actually existing' market structure in particular parts of Third World countries.

To speak of 'the market', as if there were a single integrated exchange environment, in Third World rural settings can therefore be extremely misleading. There is often more likely to be a network of micro-markets, sometimes only short distances apart, in which local power structures define the terms of trade, as well as the channels through which resources pass from lower to higher levels within the broader economy. It is not unusual to find remarkable spatial variation in prices within such situations.

Geographers have been particularly adept at identifying these idiosyncratic market contexts, which may be highly competitive in one area and highly oligopolistic in an adjacent one. Thus Carol Smith [*1977*] has drawn upon central-place theory to illustrate how, even within the restricted confines of western Guatemala, four types of 'modern' peasant market structures exist side-by-side, in four microregions each of which is tied to the national market in a different way. Some are dominated by commercial interests based outside their area, others by local trading interests. Smith concludes [*1977:   144*] that 'as more and more peasants in the world are drawn into a market economy, it becomes increasingly irrelevant to ask how much peasants are integrated by or responsive to a market economy and increasingly relevant to ask how the market that structures their economy is instituted' or structured by local historical experience.

The fact that merchants in their private capacity, and the commercial sector as an institution, are linked in varying ways to the wider system of power and production in particular regional economies implies that the fruits of economic growth (or risks of economic failure) passing through this sector can be turned to very different uses and produce a wide variety of social outcomes in different cases. As Barbara Harriss notes in her contribution to this volume, *private mercantile power may be a progressive or a regressive force in the transformation of societies.* The interests of the 'commercial sector' may lie in transforming local agricultural production or in maintaining traditional technologies and social relations; in challenging monopoly control over various kinds of resources (including political resources) or reinforcing it; in investing in industry or depositing profits in foreign bank accounts.

In other words, even a thriving private commercial sector, promoted in the rhetoric of market reform, in itself constitutes no guarantee of renewed development within the present recessionary context. Under the right circumstances, it may do so. But *the explosion of commercial activity during the past decade or so in both rural and urban areas of many Third World countries has often constituted at least as much a sign of poverty as of opportunity*. Peasant families faced by rising input and consumption costs and declining incomes, and unable to guarantee subsistence through with-drawing entirely from the market, sell more of their output, even at ruinous prices. They may also attempt to engage in some form of petty trading, again under the most primitive and unremunerative conditions imaginable. The urban poor are simultaneously turning to petty trade in record numbers, as one element in ever more complex survival strategies.

Under circumstances in which large-scale private commercial enterprise controls the key junctures between rural and urban markets, this simply increases the pool of extraordinarily cheap labour which can be drawn upon by trading businesses. The studies of Harriss and of Crow and Murshid in this volume describe the internal structure of large trading networks in which the initiative of subordinate petty traders is severely limited by ties of patronage and debt. Similar situations have been discussed by students of trade in many Latin American and African contexts. In some cases, dependent traders manage to move ahead (often through driving purchase prices from very small producers down sharply), but on the whole petty traders operating at the lower levels of networks dominated by moneylending merchants are likely to participate little if at all in any increasing profits obtained by their powerful merchant patrons. This is true not only in the rural but also in the urban segments of oligopolistic commodity markets.

There are of course an infinite variety of trading situations. The market context in some regions may be so competitive and resources so scarce that what one finds is simply a kind of commercial involution: more and more people enter the field of petty trade, working harder and harder to obtain less and less. In fact, the overall market economy under such circumstances may be shrinking. *The general economic crisis of the past decade or so has not only forced more people into trading but also, in many cases, undermined the vitality of already existing regional markets.*

Recession reduces the buying power of any potential clientele a trader may have, at the same time that it increases the costs and worsens the transport networks on which he or she must rely. Devaluation immediately raises the price of petrol and the cost of vehicles; cuts in government services worsen the roads; and attempts by public authorities to increase tax revenues are (especially in the African context) likely to be reflected in new taxes on petty trade [*Bazaara, 1991; Meagher, 1988*]. In the process, turnover of personnel within the petty trading sector is extremely high. Many students of rural life in the 1980s have documented the demise of small trading businesses in interior regions, increasing scarcity of basic products and the prevalence of ruinous price structures at both producer and consumer levels.

Under circumstances like these, what is needed to reinforce competitive and efficient private trading networks in many rural areas during a period of profound economic malaise is not a simple prescription for less public intervention, but encouragement of more effective action on the part of the state to promote marketing of basic producers' and consumers' goods under extremely difficult circumstances. This is a complex subject on which a great deal of debate has centred.

III

In the standardised discourse of market reform, state regulation of and intervention in marketing is singled out as one of the principal causes not only of agricultural stagnation but also of commercial inefficiency in rural and urban settings of many Third World countries. The criticism is grounded particularly in an analysis of food and agricultural pricing policy, which occupies a strategic place in the developmental strategies of Third World countries. Many states have played some role in setting agricultural producer prices, and in the case of export crops, these have often been held below world market prices by state marketing boards in order to increase the trading margin captured by the government upon export. This 'tax' on producers has formed an important part of public revenue.

At the same time, state marketing boards or food corporations have usually made some effort to buy basic grains at relatively low prices in order to feed a growing urban population at the least possible cost. This has contributed further to a systematic bias against agriculture, mitigated to some extent by subsidies on farm inputs and marketing services which have cheapend the cost of production for groups more closely integrated into the market. Subsidies lowering the consumer price of basic foodstuffs in major urban areas have also increased the relative advantage of urban over rural people.

A general diagnosis of rural disadvantage, growing out of mistaken public policy, has thus often been in order. Relative prices have frequently been set against agriculture, and state marketing agencies have played a role in extracting resources from agricultural producers, to be transferred to urban-industrial sectors or simply to be squandered through corruption. Robert Bates [1981], Michael Lipton [1977] and others have explored the political economy of urban bias in convincing detail.[6]

As usual in the complicated world of real markets, however, the picture is never as simple as it seems. To begin with, *public pricing policy – like most other areas of public policy – has had in the past and still has many purposes, some of which are thoroughly contradictory*. The driving forces of policy-making are political, not technical, and they produce incongruous results. Thus while a number of pricing measures may penalise rural people, others represent attempts to improve their position in extremely imperfect markets.

One of these measures is pan-territorial pricing, which establishes a single guaranteed price for certain farm products throughout the national territory. Such an effort can be extremely costly if it supports producer prices in distant farming regions, where the cost of transport to any major market is high. In times of economic crisis, this is difficult for governments to sustain. But such programmes, implemented through state-run buying stations and often supported financially by foreign donors, have provided indispensable support for rural development efforts in many relatively remote areas of Third World countries, where market prices would not justify commercial production. As Deborah Bryceson notes in her contribution to this volume, they have represented a commitment to 'spatial egalitarianism', even in countries criticised for strong urban bias in certain aspects of the pricing structure.

The assumption that the intervention of the state in rural marketing is *necessarily* damaging to rural people is therefore confirmed neither by logic nor by experience. The efforts of the Grain Marketing Board of the government of Zimbabwe, for example, stand behind the much-lauded expansion of maize production in communal farming areas over the past few years. Without the provision of subsidised marketing services, small farmers could not have benefitted from increased yields [*Amin, 1992*]. More generally, the maintenance of agricultural support prices, even at relatively low levels, protects farm families in many Third World countries (as in the industrialised nations) from extreme variation in income associated with innumerable factors, ranging from unpredictable climate to oligopolistic trading practices.

Adjustment-related attempts to remove such equilibrium-'distorting' mechanisms as support prices can be justified as emergency measures forced upon governments by economic crisis. But to urge that these steps be taken on technical or ideological grounds – as an inherently proper reinstitution of 'free market forces' – and that macroeconomic policy reform of this kind will automatically benefit rural people, is disingenuous. *The livelihood of farming families can be devastated by loss of access to support prices and associated state-run marketing services, as has been the case over wide areas of Latin America and Africa during the past decade.*

Whether state intervention in agricultural markets benefits or harms rural people in fact depends at least as much on the degree of compulsion associated with public marketing programmes as on the level of the official price and its relation to alternatives in the unregulated market. *Official crop pricing programmes are likely to favour producers most when they are available to all on a discretionary basis. They favour producers least when delivery at the fixed price is mandatory*; and in fact, the neoliberal stereotype of harmful state intervention in agricultural markets is drawn from reference to the latter case, not the former.

Experience throughout the Third World has shown that attempts on the part of national governments to ban private commerce in certain basic products and to create a single official channel for trade through state marketing boards tend to be politically and economically costly, and finally unsustainable. Monopoly control over the purchase of farm products, when exercised by the state, is as likely to harm 'captive' sellers as is the exercise of monopoly control by private traders. It constitutes the mechanism through which governments can enforce artifically low prices, as emphasised in discussions on urban bias; and it provides fertile ground for corruption.

To illustrate the differential effects which state marketing programmes can have on various groups of rural producers, depending upon the characteristics of local markets and the degree of coercion or voluntarism involved in the official programme, it is useful to refer briefly to the case of Mexico. In that country, a complex structure of market regulation was developed during the postwar period to perform a wide range of functions, from regulating producer and consumer prices for certain basic products to ensuring the supply of grain throughout the national territory. This effort never involved the prohibition of private trade or the legal imposition of a governmental monopoly. The expressed intention of the government has always been to correct market forces – to regulate at the margin – not to eliminate the market altogether.

Nevertheless the functioning of the agricultural credit system created a *de facto* public-sector monopoly on crops produced by agrarian reform beneficiaries with official financing. As was later to prove the case in a number of developing countries, loans extended by the state-run rural bank were guaranteed against the purchase of borrowers' crops. Given the need to support and develop peasant agriculture, and disinterest in this venture on the part of private enterprise, such an arrangement seemed logical and necessary. Over the long run, however, it fell prey to corruption and became an instrument for extracting resources from a captive farming sector. The level of support prices at which crops were acquired by the official rural bank was often lower than that prevailing in regional markets; and producers in these developing commercial areas therefore began a long struggle to free themselves from the state-run trading system, so that they could bargain independently.

This, however, is only half of the picture. While selling at the official price proved detrimental to the interests of a sector of small commercial farmers operating within the framework of a *de facto* state-controlled monopoly on the purchase of certain crops (financed through the official credit system), access to the same support price was an alternative much in demand in more backward areas of rural Mexico. Plagued by interlocking private markets which held them in perpetual debt, the poorer peasantry of remote regions throughout the Mexican countryside insistently requested the extension of state trading programmes into disadvantaged areas, in order to challenge exploitative local monopolies. In fact, organisations of poorer rural producers and consumers have fought long battles – often at the cost of lives – to establish officially-sponsored marketing cooperatives in their localities.

The experience of the peasantry in such backward regions of Mexico must be followed a step further in order to underline the complexity of relations between public and private sectors in real rural settings: even when local people were successful in breaching the economic and political barriers which traditionally maintained their dependence on local political bosses and moneylending traders, and even when they gained outside allies who could support the establishment of marketing cooperatives in their communities, this was in no sense a guarantee that the potential benefits of the new arrangement would ultimately be realised. The struggle for control of the local market (and for control of local livelihood) was played out within ideosyncratic political arenas. In some cases, peasant producers were successful in using the power of regional and national allies (in the state-run marketing agency and the government) to alter the terms of trade and power in their communities. In others, the marketing programme was taken over by the traditional landholding and merchant elite, perhaps in collusion with employees of the national marketing programme.[7]

The point to be made is that when subject to empirical scrutiny, *the state is no more a single entity than the market, and that economic and political structures blend together at the local level in rural areas of the Third World to create exchange environments which cannot be understood by simply refering to general characteristics of state and market in the country*. This assertion is associated with another, at a more general level: in the last analysis, conceptualising state and market as isolated – or opposite – entities (much less attributing to either a positive or negative connotation) is likely to encourage both bad social science and bad social policy.

IV

The tendency throughout the 1980s for the discourse on reform to revolve around a supposed state-market dichotomy, and to abstract both state and market from the society which forms their common base, has furthered a number of misconceptions. In the first place, the policy debate has been so dominated by strong neoliberal concern with 'getting the state out of marketing' (countered by strong nationalist concern with maintaining a state presence in that field) that *official market intervention in Third World countries has been made to appear far more widespread and pervasive than it actually is or has been.* In fact, with the exception of consolidated socialist economies, even the most concerted efforts of Third World governments to outlaw private commerce or regulate trade have encompassed an extremely small part of the real national market. Greatest control has been exercised in the case of export crops. But in the case of grain and other staple crops, attempts by African governments to monopolise trade have never been more than partially effective;[8] and (with the exception of Cuba) private trade has never been outlawed in Latin America at all.

In the second place, *this debate has often assumed a life of its own, increasingly unrelated to the real world of marketing* for both staple and commercial crops. As governments and foreign advisors or creditors have argued endlessly about the technicalities of market reform, local people in many countries have continued to meet immediate needs through developing new modalities of exchange. Deborah Bryceson notes, for example, that during the 1980s private grain markets developed so consistently in Tanzania, even within the context of nominally all-pervasive governmental regulation, that the intense high-level debate on the merits of market liberalisation in that country in fact proved increasingly irrelevant.

Finally, when needed policy reforms are carried out in states which have indeed imposed unrealistic regulations on trade, or exerted monopoly control over certain products, the ideological character of the state/market debate can to some extent obscure both the underlying social processes contributing to reform and the enduring problems of exchange which will remain even after the policy reform process has been completed.

This is particularly likely in the case of Third World socialist countries. As Peter Utting argues in the concluding chapter of this volume, trade liberalisation in such settings can only partially be explained within a formalistic macroeconomic and macropolitical framework. The process of reform advances not only as a technocratic response to economic constraints, or as a political response to immediate challenge, or even as an ideological shift, but also because medium-term changes in social organisation at the grassroots make restructuring unavoidable.

The Nicaraguan experience analysed by Utting also provides a clear example of the fact that *basic problems of provisioning and market regulation do not disappear simply because structures of more or less pervasive official control over certain areas of exchange are dismantled.* In situations of deep economic crisis, often aggravated by war or civil strife, in which production of basic staples may be declining and markets may be increasingly disarticulated, eliminating certain costly or unworkable programmes or trade policies may prove more useful as a means to balance the budget than as a way to ensure that masses of people will have access to basic goods. After old strategies are discarded, the challenge of building new ones remains.

V

There is, then, an urgent need for market reform throughout the Third World. But this is not a task to which any standard set of policy prescriptions can be applied. In some cases, exploitative structures of private commerce hold large numbers of people in virtual bondage; in others, there is no private market to speak of at all. In some cases, small farmers and traders must be freed from state tutelage; in others, they must gain access to state support. There are governments which extract too much from the countryside and governments which extract too little. There are places where rural and urban interests clash sharply and places where they do not.

Market reform will have to be worked out pragmatically, on the ground. And as it is, basic structural dilemmas of livelihood and provisioning within Third World societies must be confronted.[9] These dilemmas appear again and again in the following pages.

NOTES

1. Recent calls for new work on 'real markets' can be found in Bernstein [1989]; Harriss [1984]; Hewitt de Alcántara [1989]; Mackintosh [1990].
2. A comprehensive review of developments in sub-Saharan African countries by Lionel Demery and Tony Addison [1987, p. 193] 'cast serious doubt on any presumption that the pro-agriculture policy conditionality of the World Bank and IMF will improve food security in SSA in the foreseeable future'. And Kydd and Scarborough [1988: 26] concluded that 'implementation [of reforms] has raised as many new problems as it has solved'.
    For Latin America, see Twomey [1989]; and Schejtman [1988].
3. Although it is the goal of reformers in Eastern Europe and the Soviet Union to construct modern consumer societies of a Western European or American type, the social reality of some areas is in fact closer to that of some Third World countries; and the possibility should therefore not be overlooked that the kinds of markets which emerge in rural areas will bear considerable resemblance to one of the variants of market organisation in developing nations.
4. For a discussion of the concept of interface see Long [1989].
5. Andrew Pearse [1975] provided an exceptionally clear analysis of this process in his book on the Latin American peasantry. See also Bohannan and Dalton [1962].
6. For a Latin American analysis of urban bias, see Hewitt de Alcántara [1976].
7. Essays on these experiences can be found in Hewitt de Alcántara [1992].
8. According to one estimate, cited by Green [1989; 40], less than 10 per cent of all domestic

food production in Africa, and less than one-third of all marketed food production, might have been handled through official channels around the turn of the 1980s. Such figures are, of course, extremely debatable since no reliable statistics exist in large areas of rural Africa (or Latin America).

9. For a useful discussion of these issues, see the last chapter of the book by Solon Barraclough [*1991*] on food strategies in Africa, Asia and Latin America.

REFERENCES

Amin, N., 1992, 'State and Peasantry in Zimbabwe since Independence', *European Journal of Development Research*, Vol. 4, No. 1.

Arhin, K., Hesp, P. and L. van der Laan, 1985, *Marketing Boards in Tropical Africa*, London: Routledge Kegan Paul.

Bhaduri, A., 1986, 'Forced Commerce and Agrarian Change', *World Development*, Vol. 14, No. 2.

Barraclough, S., 1991, *An End to Hunger? The Social Origins of Food Strategies*, London: Zed/UNRISD/South Centre.

Bates, R., 1981, *States and Markets in Tropical Africa*, Berkeley, CA: University of California Press.

Bazaara, N., 1991, 'Structural Adjustment Programmes: The Liberalisation of Food Markets and Social Change in Uganda', final version of a paper prepared for the Seminar on Food Pricing and Marketing Reform, UNRISD, Geneva, 20-22 Nov. 1989.

Bohannan, P., and G. Dalton (eds.), 1962, *Markets in Africa*, Evanston, IL: Northwestern University Press.

Bernstein, H., 1989, *Agricultural 'Modernisation' in the Era of Structural Adjustment*, Development Policy and Practice Discussion Paper No. 16, Milton Keynes: Open University.

Commander, S., Ndoye, O. and I. Ouedrago, 1989, 'Senegal, 1979-1988', in S. Commander (ed.), *Structural Adjustment and Agriculture*, London: Overseas Development Institute/ James Currey.

Delaine, G., L. Demery et al., 1992, *The Social Dimensions of Adjustment Integrated Survey: A Survey to Measure Poverty and Understand the Effects of Policy Change on Households*, Social Dimensions of Adjustment in Sub Saharan Africa Working Paper No. 14, Washington, DC: World Bank.

Demery, L. and T. Addison, 1987, 'Food Insecurity and Adjustment Policies in Sub Saharan Africa: A Review of the Evidence', *Development Policy Review*, Vol. 5.

Ghai, D. (ed), 1991, *The IMF and the South: The Social Impact of Crisis and Adjustment*, London: Zed/UNRISD/ISER.

Green, R., 1989, 'Articulating Stabilisation Programmes and Structural Adjustment: Sub Saharan Africa', in S. Commander (ed.), *Structural Adjustment and Agriculture*, London: Overseas Development Institute/James Currey.

Harrigan, J., 1988, 'Malawi: The Impact of Pricing Policy on Smallholder Agriculture, 1971-1988', *Development Policy Review*, Vol. 6, No. 4.

Harriss, B., 1984, *State and Market*, New Delhi: Concept Publishing Co.

Hewitt de Alcántara, C., 1976, *Modernizing Mexican Agriculture*, Geneva: United Nations Research Institute for Social Development.

Hewitt de Alcántara, C., 1989, 'Food Pricing and Marketing Reform: Social and Political Issues', Paper prepared for the Seminar on Food Pricing and Marketing Reform, UNRISD, Geneva, 20-22 Nov. 1989.

Hewitt de Alcántara, C. (ed.), 1992, *Reestructuración económica y subsistencia rural*, Mexico City: El Colegio de México/Centro Tepoztlán/UNRISD; summarised in English in *Economic Restructuring and Rural Subsistence in Mexico: Maize and the Crisis of the 1980s*, Discussion Paper No. 31, Geneva: UNRISD.

Igbedioh, S., 1990, 'Macroeconomic Adjustment, Food Availability and Nutrition Status in Nigeria: A Look at the 1990s', *Food Policy*, Vol.15, No. 6.

Kydd, J., 1986, 'Changes in Zambian Agricultural Policy since 1983: Problems of Liberalization and Agrarianization', *Development Policy Review*, Vol. 4.

Kydd, J. and V. Scarborough, 1988, 'Liberalisation and Privatisation in Sub Saharn African Food Marketing: A Survey of the Issues', paper prepared for the Overseas Development National Resources Institute of the United Kingdom.

Lipton, M., 1977, *Why Poor People Stay Poor: Urban Bias in World Development*, London: Temple Smith.

Lipton, M., 1987, 'Limits of Price Policy for Agriculture: Which Way for the World Bank', *Development Policy Review*, Vol. 5.

Long, N. (ed.), 1989, *Encounters at the Interface: A Perspective on Social Discontinuities in Rural Development*, Wageningen: Agricultural University of Wageningen.

Mackintosh, M., 1986, *Agricultural Marketing and Socialist Accumulation: A Case Study of Maize Marketing in Mozambique*, Development Policy and Practice Working Paper No. 1, Milton Keynes: Open University.

Mackintosh, M., 1990, 'Abstract Markets and Real Needs', in H. Bernstein, B. Crow *et al.* (eds.), *The Food Question*, London: Earthscan.

Meagher, K., 1988, 'The Market in the Lived Economy: A Report on the Dynamic of Official and Parallel Market Activities in Arua District, Uganda', unpublished paper, Sussex: Institute of Development Studies of the University of Sussex.

Pearse, A., 1975, *The Latin American Peasant*, London: Frank Cass.

Pinstrup-Andersen, Per, 1989, 'Government Policy, Food Security and Nutrition in Sub Saharan Africa', PEW/Cornell Lecture Series on Food and Nutrition Policy, Ithaca: Cornell Food and Nutrition Policy Programme.

Polanyi, K., 1957, *The Great Transformation*, Boston: Beacon Press.

Pottier, J., 1989, 'Food Security in Rwanda', Paper prepared for the Seminar on Food Pricing and Marketing Reform, UNRISD, Geneva, 20-22 Nov. 1989.

Robinson, J., 1977, 'What Are the Questions', *Journal of Economic Literature*, Vol. 15, No. 4.

Sahn, D. and J. Arulpragasam, 1991, 'The Stagnation of Smallholder Agriculture in Malawi: A Decade of Structural Adjustment', *Food Policy*, Vol. 16, No. 3.

Schejtman, A., 1988, 'La seguridad alimentaria: Tendencias e impacto de la crisis', *Revista de la CEPAL*, No. 36.

Sen, A., 1981, *Poverty and Famines: An Essay on Entitlement and Deprivation*, Oxford: Clarendon Press.

Smith, C., 1977, 'How Marketing Systems Affect Economic Opportunity in Agrarian Societies', in R. Halperin and J. Dow (eds.), *Peasant Livelihood*, New York: St. Martins.

Spoor, M., 1991, *The State and Domestic Agricultural Markets in Developing Countries: The Case of Nicaragua under Sandinista Rule (1979-1990)*, Unpublished Ph. D. thesis, University of Amsterdam.

Taylor, L., 1988, *Varieties of Stabilization Experience*, Oxford: Clarendon.

Twomey, M., 1989, 'The Debt Crisis and Latin American Agriculture', *The Journal of Developing Areas*, Vol. 23.

World Bank, 1981, *Accelerated Development in Sub Saharan Africa: An Agenda for Action*, Washington: World Bank.

World Bank, 1986, *World Development Report*, 1986, Oxford: Oxford University Press.

Paths of Authority: Roads, the State and the Market in Eastern Zaire

JAMES FAIRHEAD

Markets for land, labour and goods in rural Zaire are embedded in autocratic and often corrupt local power domains which have been strengthened by economic crisis and concomitant structural adjustment policies. To talk of 'the market' in this context is as meaningless as to talk of 'the state'. The following article focuses on efforts to facilitate market integration through roadbuilding in rural areas, and on the way the advancing market affects the life chances of different local groups.

When regional planners and development agents glance at their maps of Kivu, in Eastern Zaire, they see the road network standing out in bold red ink, covering the entire region. The contrast between the map's optimistic promise and what the planners know to be reality is a potent reminder of economic decline and what has come to be known as the *mal Zairois*.

Although at independence in 1960 Zaire was the second most industrialised country in Africa, containing incredibly rich natural resources across a vast expanse of territory, its history has been a tragic one. Economic and educational opportunities for the people of Zaire were rigorously limited by the Belgian colonial administration; and after the departure of the Belgians, struggle among national factions for political and economic control degenerated into a civil war which lasted until 1967. Turmoil wrecked the economy and destroyed the institutional, administrative and legal structure.

James Fairhead, School of Oriental and African Studies, London University. Fieldwork, carried out in Kivu between October 1986 and June 1988, was funded by the Economic and Social Research Council of Great Britain (A00428524351), and was carried out in co-operation with both the Centro Internacional de Agricultura Tropical (CIAT), through their Programme Regional pour l'Amélioration du Haricot dans la Région des Grands Lacs, and the Centre de Développement Rural (CEDERU). A return visit was made during November 1989. Grateful acknowledgement is made to these institutions, and to the many Citoyens and Citoyennes in Zaire who helped him in the field. None of them is in any way responsible for errors of fact or interpretation. The author would also like to thank UNRISD seminar participants for their comments on the first draft of this article and Cynthia Hewitt de Alcántara and Melissa Leach for their later comments and suggestions.

Therefore although the economy managed to flourish for a few years at the turn of the 1970s, buoyed by high commodity prices, the foundations of economic prosperity for rural Zairians had crumbled.

In 1973 foreign investments were 'Zairianised' and imported oil prices rose; and in 1974 the price of the country's principal mineral export (copper) collapsed. Financial reserves were rapidly depleted, and in 1975 Zaire defaulted on its debt for the first time.[1] This was followed by an agreement with the IMF in 1976, in which help in rescheduling debt and a standby loan were offered in exchange for devaluation, a cut in imports and government spending, and increased investment in agriculture. That such pledges had little effect is illustrated by the fact that debt was rescheduled again in 1977, 1979, 1980, 1981, and 1983.

In 1983, Zaire and the IMF agreed on a standby loan agreement which was conditional upon adoption of a standard structural adjustment package: massive devaluation, decontrol of producer prices (especially in the agricultural sector), reduction of public spending, trade liberalisation and revision of customs duties. Until 1986, creditors praised themselves (and Zaire) for their programme. Reform success was, however, premised on hopes for increased commodity prices and international aid, neither of which was forthcoming. Debt service rose from 11 percent of government expenditure in 1982 to 56 percent in 1985, and the government abandoned the adjustment reform programme in 1986 and 1987. Through default and rescheduling the official debt continued to rise, from 5.5 billion US dollars in 1985 to 8.5 billion in 1989 [*Kawata, 1989*]. Needless to say, the impact of the continuing crisis on levels of living, most particularly for those employed in the public sector, has been severe.

The real problems of economic reorganisation underlying the crisis are inextricably bound up with the nature of Zairian society and politics. The concept of 'state' authority has in fact always been problematic when applied to the area now contained within Zaire. The sheer size of the territory has constituted a brake on centralised control and favoured a kind of indirect exercise of authority through local intermediaries with wide and often despotic power over the population.

Personalistic, almost feudal control was in the first instance a fundamental trait of early Belgian colonialism. From 1895 until 1908, the Congo Free State was in fact a personal holding of King Leopold of Belgium; and appropriation of the labour, produce and taxes of those most easily subjugated was ensured through brutal treatment, including enslavement or threatened enslavement. Political control over regions in the 'interior', however, was most often minimal. Eventually, public outcry in Europe forced the Belgian government to assume responsibility for the territory, and the new administration and army of the Belgian Congo were gradually able to widen their area of control through creating the structures of indirect rule which persist, to a greater or lesser degree, up to the present day.

Between the colonial administration and the populace, pliable intermediary Paramount Chiefs were installed with the influence necessary to force the population to accept orders and remain obedient. In Kivu, these chiefs, who rule over their *Collectivité*, were termed *Mwami* (plural *Bami*). Today they head what can euphemistically be called a 'traditional' political hierarchy consisting of sub-chiefs (*Chef de Groupement*), locality chiefs (*Chef de Localité*), and village chiefs (*Kapita*). *Bami*, reinforced by the territorial, regional and national administration above them, by the national army and their own police force, by their lucrative sale of chiefdom land to Europeans, by their ability forcibly to recruit labour, and by their control over ivory and other trade, acquired far greater wealth and power over the population than ever before.

In the *Collectivité* of Bwisha in the Zone of Rutshuru, as elsewhere in Kivu, this powerful coercive coalition of state administrators, traditional administrators, army, police, and colonial entrepreneurs (in coffee, tea and quinine plantations) had a virtualy free hand over many years to expropriate land from cultivators, to extort heavy taxes, and to recruit labour for work in the plantations, road building and infrastructure.

It took war-related famine during the 1940s to modify the terms of repression. The Belgian colonial administration declared labour to be free and attempted to curtail the authority of *Bami*, commercial plantations and national parks, which were often allied in corrupt and illegal ways [*Mendiaux, 1956; Nzabandora, 1984*]. The colonial administration was, however, weak in relation to these interest groups. In consequence, the programme intended to strengthen the power of the population (and administration) relative to traditional chiefs and capital, and to introduce local democracy, progressed slowly. New laws were still relatively ineffective at independence in 1960.

In some regions, like Bwisha, the freeing of labour did benefit ordinary people during the 1950s reform period and there was some success in curtailing the power of the *Bami*. During the anarchic period between 1960 and 1967, however, this trend was definitively reversed. Since that time, the chiefs have regained and reinforced their 'feudal' power, both as landlords and in alliance with investors, including national politicians. When foreign plantation capital was 'Zairianised' in 1973, for example, many of the spoils were taken by *Bami* and their sub-chiefs. And with the deepening economic crisis, decline in central financing of regional and local state government has forced state personnel, including the army, to rely on *Bami* and corruption for finance and income. The weakness of central authorities is exacerbated by the fact that state posts involve limited tenure, to prevent state bureaucrats from building close and politically threatening alliances with local populations. Finally, the rhetoric of *authenticité* has favoured 'traditional' feudal leaders over modern 'state' ones.

In sum, therefore, the institution of 'the state' in Zaire may be terrifying and strong for the local population, but its control from the centre is actually very weak [*Schatzberg, 1988*]. Structural adjustment policies designed to 'roll the state back' are wrong to presuppose that the central state could exercise such control, even if its leaders had the political will to exert it [*Thomas and Reintsma, 1989*]. Furthermore, critics of structural adjustment who have argued that the IMF and Work Bank 'now manage each country entirely' by imposing staff and vetting monetary, fiscal, tariff, trade and investment policies, and that this is the 'recolonization of Africa' [*Onimode, 1987*], would seem vastly to overestimate the role of the centre (be it Zairian or IMF) in managing the state, while significantly underestimating the importance of the 'second' or parallel economy [*MacGaffey, 1987*] and of 'second' or 'parallel' polities.

To talk of 'the market' in Zaire is as problematic as to talk of 'the state'. Just as the state is ultimately made up of territorially-based hierarchies of power, so too one finds that markets for land, labour and goods are locally bound, politically managed and thus anything but free. This 'underdevelopment' of the market is perceived by foreign advisors as a concomitant of the physical isolation and technological backwardness of rural people. In addition to mounting programmes which attempt to provide smallholder credit, extension services and access to new production inputs, then, the series of agricultural development efforts set in motion with international assistance over the past few decades – including the most recent efforts to bolster economic 'adjustment' through the promotion of agricultural growth – almost always has to consider the question of how to facilitate market integration through improving the rural communications network.

In 1972, the World Bank was instrumental in creating the Zairian road-building parastatal, Office des Routes; and in recent years money has continued to be channelled toward modernising transport, as a concomitant of project-based investment in agricultural extension and credit, and as support for programmes of producer price reform. As of 1984, the Bank had allocated US$237 million to road and rail rehabilitation; and a donors' meeting held in March of the following year 'dealt exclusively with the transport sector' [*Leslie, 1987: 103*].

But what is the relation between expanding road networks, markets and rural 'development' in a context like that of Zaire? What kind of a market has been created in relatively isolated rural areas over the past few decades? Whose interests does the expanding road network serve and what kind of social change is promoted?

It is the contention of this article that questions like these must be answered very specifically, through reference to the evolution of livelihood strategies within particular rural environments over a substantial period of time. Furthermore, the development of the market for goods (and most importantly for food) must be examined as it interacts with changes in the markets for land and labour. Widening road networks affect the entire structure of resources available to various kinds of people, not simply the price of traded commodities. And even more important, perhaps, the impact of the market is felt not only among households (promoting social stratification and the coalescence of classes) but within them. Members of households experience market changes differently, with implications for the structure and meaning of community and family life.

A VIEW FROM BELOW: ROADS AS PATHS OF AUTHORITY

In the village in Eastern Zaire where I lived for 20 months between 1986 and 1988, roads were a big issue. Six kilometres from the village, down in the base of the Rift Valley which it overlooks, there is an important road, opened in 1958, which links the arterial Goma–Kisangani road with Uganda. Villages nearby have recently built access roads to this main road, and some people in Kakoma[2] wanted do the same. Financial and technical assistance for road building was available from Programme Kivu (supported by the European Economic Community) and from Italian mission funds. Evidence from surrounding villages suggested that a road would improve the chances of establishing a market place in the village and attract more traders, encouraging higher producer prices and cheaper consumer ones. A nearby village had built an access road in 1984 and by 1986 had a thriving weekly market. Despite such benefits, however, there were clear differences of opinion concerning the advisability of constructing a road.

Divided interests were generated by concerns far broader than those of price or expanding economic opportunity. It should be understood at the outset that roads link the village with the outside world in a way which is qualitatively different from the links implied by the flow of goods and people along local pathways. From colonial times, roads were associated with the exercise of power by the state or the chiefs: forced labour was recruited to build them, personal movement along them was taxed and controlled, and indigenous land near them was expropriated for plantations and mission stations. In practice, this situation has changed little over the post-independence period. Roads still have to be built and maintained at vast labour expense. Roads make the surrounding land more attractive for commercial farming, and thus more valuable; and this still encourages land appropriation by the powerful. And roads are still the site of forced exactions which make the ideal conception of the 'free market' of relatively limited utility in rural Zaire.

Direct Exaction

Many men are in fact afraid to walk along roads in Bwisha because they are likely to be robbed there by political *cadres*, the police of the *Mwami* and *Chef de Groupement*, the gendarmes, and the soldiers, all of whom tend to stay near roads when not on other duties. Robbery is often overt, although it can also be camouflaged through trumped-up charges. For example, each man in the village must carry receipts for tax payments and proof that he has voted, as well as a *Carte pour Citoyen*. Receipts, however, often cost more than the amount received, and identity cards are kept unavailable by the local authorities. Since men without these documents are fined on the spot and/or threatened with imprisonment if they are checked, and since checks on the road are frequent, the solution chosen by many is to avoid the roads.

Some men and all women are, however, protected from such banditry and hence consider roads more positively. Officials, who are rarely certain of their contextual authority over the strangers they rob, tend neither to approach nor to exact tribute from those who give the appearance of 'position', or those who can prove it. This means that the three primary school teachers, the five members of the Village Committee of the *Mouvement Populaire de la Révolution* (MPR), the village chief and his two deputies (all of whom are state functionaries and bear special identity cards) are protected. To show this, they often wear a Party badge when walking on the road.

Equally, three Protestant and three Catholic church officials are relatively immune from extortion, and the churches foster powerful political connections which protect the general congregation somewhat as well. For men, this is a very real reason for joining the church. Since Catholic and Baptist (CEBK) missionaries have good contacts with the *Commissaire de Zone*, the *Mwami*, and the military, they are even able to respond to complaints of the faithful by having offending soldiers arrested and stolen goods returned. Under such circumstances, it is not hard to understand the protective value some villagers accord to carrying bibles and wearing large crucifixes when journeying.

Others who can prove exemption from compulsory community labour (*solongo*, to be discussed below) also seem to enjoy relative immunity from direct expropriation by bandits on the road. Those who have proof of accredited employment have such exemption documents, as do those who work in 'development'. The latter group includes three members of a Village

Development Committee constituted in the framework of a local rural development centre, and two Red Cross paramedical health workers.

It should be noted that such immunity from extortion on the roads parallels forms of protection which have long been characteristic of rural life in Zaire. During pre-colonial and early colonial times, villagers derived similar security from membership in a patrikin-based community (*umuryango*, normally consisting of between 100 and 1,000 people) outside of which anyone could become the victim of anyone else. During the colonial period, employment in the plantations (and elsewhere) gave workers immunity from recruitment into other areas of forced labour, including road building. There has always been an important distinction between those who have protective ties or documents, showing them to be part of a greater community, and those who do not.

About a quarter of the men in the village where I lived can avoid direct expropriation and find it relatively safe to use the roads. Church officials of all denominations, school teachers, development workers and health workers, form a distinct group of common outlook. Not surprisingly they are also the wealthier villagers. Wealth makes it easier to gain positions of protection and vice versa.

Women have a different experience. They are relatively free of direct expropriation on the roads and in markets. They resent illegal taxation strongly, and can be very aggressive towards officials who attempt to impose it. Women tend to walk to market in groups and physically to protect each other against the officials they encounter on their journeys. Newbury has documented a revolt by women over increased taxes elsewhere in Kivu, and shows how, just as in Bwisha, their liberty gives them certain marketing advantages over men:

> ... men 'hide behind women' in marketing their peanuts. Men send women to carry peanuts to market these days (say the women) for reasons of security. A man who has just received 150 zaires or more for a *mbweka* of peanuts is fair game for gendarmes who prowl about Bulambika market seeking potential victims to be relieved of their earnings on the basis of some trumped-up charge. Alternatively a man with money in his pocket at market finds that this disappears quickly when friends and relatives call on him to buy them drinks. These problems do not arise when women carry peanuts to the market [*1984b: 46–7*].

Labour Exactions

In order to understand the differential distribution of benefits and dis-benefits associated with the construction of the road, the institution of *solongo*, or unpaid community labour, must also be briefly discussed. For pre-colonial patrikin communities, *solongo* was labour tribute which a newcomer would give to his hosts. Under Belgian rule, however, it became the compulsory labour (60 days/year, raised to 120 days/year during the Second World War) exacted from all those without accredited employment. *Solongo* is thus a form of labour tribute to the powerful, and not community labour in any meaningful sense of the term.

Solongo is organised by representatives of the traditional and state hierarchy: the village chief (*Kapita*) and his seniors, and the president of a village *comité de base* of the MPR. These coexisting political structures overlap (often competitively) in jurisdiction, and there are frequent disputes over the rights of each to *corvée* labour. Common *solongo* tasks include cultivating the fields of the *Mwami* and his sub-chiefs (including the village *Kapita*), building and maintaining their houses, building and maintaining roads, and on rare occasions, maintaining social infrastructure such as schools and clinics. Superiors justify their private use of 'state' labour by claiming that it is payment for what are otherwise unpaid posts. Obviously, such a situation allows chiefs to translate political power into economic gain.

There are, however, ways to avoid the *corvée*. The *Kapita* permits relatives, friends and respected men to evade normal *solongo* work in Bwisha if they pay 20 litres of banana wine and a chicken. This reduces the number who do *solongo* to twenty or so men who are young and poor. Nevertheless payment of tribute to chiefs signifies powerlessness on the part of the petitioner and consequent dependence on the continuing goodwill of the chief. Those who avoid *solongo* in this way cannot refuse the subsequent frequent supplementary demands which the *Kapita* makes, and life becomes financially insecure.

Men who bribe the *Kapita* nevertheless gain a certain independence from the state within the village. They, and the Kapita, realise that if a road were built to the village, the power of the Kapita would wane, and with it their unofficial exemption. The road would permit those in higher political positions living outside the village to take more direct control over village affairs, expropriate labour directly, and manage lucrative tribunals, while at the moment higher authorities have only indirect, inefficient control via the village chief.

Women are exempt from *solongo*. On one occasion, they successfully organised themselves against it when forced to plant cassava for the *Chef de Groupement*. Angry and worried by the precedent, they cut the nodes (eyes) off the cassava stems which they planted. The crop did not grow. It is said that the astonished chief suspects sorcery to this day, and he has not forced the women to work again.

In summary, many of those who will have to build the road are not in favour of road building, as they would effectively be building the vehicle of their own oppression. As during colonial times, when roads were built by the forced labour of men unfortunate enough to be unable to escape recruitment, the burden of road building falls on unprotected men. This includes people who do *solongo* at present (young, poor, powerless men, especially recent immigrants without family contacts in the village) and the many who avoid *solongo* because of their position relative to the chiefs (better placed men without official institutional jobs). Only those men who are immune from *solongo* and hence immune from road building, who pursue their own lives with some measure of security, and whose authority may actually be increased by better access to missionaries, development personnel and traders, favour road building. It is these people who development experts are likely to meet. Women, who are rarely robbed on roads, who are exempt from building them, and who presently suffer in carrying produce long distances to market, seem to side with the protected men on this issue. They do not necessarily see eye to eye with their husbands.

Expropriation of Land

In spite of deepening economic crisis in Zaire, there has been a great increase in demand on the part of entrepreneurs and politicians for large tracts of plantation land during the 1980s [*Katuala Kaba et al., 1986*], and this demand is now being accentuated by infrastructural improvements [*Schoepf and Schoepf, 1987*]. As inflation erodes the value of stored money and as trade is a relatively risky and difficult occupation, those in politically superior positions currently prefer to store and reproduce wealth in cattle and in land, that is, in cattle ranching. At the same time, infrastructural decay and the collapse of coffee prices has also led plantation owners to uproot coffee and switch to cattle. Ranching is easy, less risky and lucrative. There is a large, experienced and skilled local Batutsi workforce. At the same time, gaining control over land serves to gain greater control over labour, to force down wage rates and pass the burden of economic decline on to a more securely tied labour force.

In Kivu, livestock is now almost the only profitable investment; and its profitability is increased by aid organisations. Canadians have funded the construction of a modern abattoir which has improved meat processing; and with the development of air freight, Kivu cattle ranchers now have access to the Kinshasa market. In tandem, FAO, the Canadian-funded ACOGENOKI, and the American Peace Corps have all invested heavily in the development of cattle ranching. They provide education, advice and direct inputs to improve pasture management and veterinary care. And loans from commercial and development banks (like the Agricultural Credit

Bank) have been made available at preferential interest rates to well placed investors in livestock [*Schoepf and Schoepf, 1987*]. President Mobutu himself has castigated the Agricultural Credit Bank (partially funded by the World Bank) for not meeting the needs of peasants, and for favouring the wealthy who expropriate land (see the Kivu newspaper ELIMA, 8/12/84).

The people of Bwisha have recent experience with the expansion of large landholdings across their village lands. In 1984, the owner of the massive ex-colonial plantation which borders on the village extended the border of his holding by about 500 yards. He claimed that the original borders (defined on maps in the land registration office far away in Bukavu) were further into the village than the markers (concrete slabs) showed. He asserted that the villagers had encroached on the plantation and moved its boundary markers. This was falsification. The plantation owner was well connected and wealthy, and, villagers say, was able to pay off a surveyor and others to validate his claim. His action reduced the land area of the village by about a quarter. Many people found their houses and fields incorporated within the new boundary; and they subsequently faced the choice of continuing to live in the plantation and giving up both one day a week's labour and their autonomy to it, or moving out. They moved out, charging that the plantation was purposefully extended to gain authority over them, as the owner wanted free labour.

ADMINISTRATION PROLIFERATION AND DECENTRALISATION

Changes in the balance of power between regional and local administrators and public employees, on the one hand, and the central government on the other, are further exacerbating the insecurity of unprotected cultivators in many regions of Zaire. The financial crisis of the state and the need for structural adjustment have made decentralisation a necessity for the government. Regions have been granted more autonomy, and local administrative units have been told to look after themselves as the central government can no longer afford to fund their activities [*Leslie, 1987: 74; Newbury, 1984a: 112–15*].

At the same time, decentralisation has been accompanied by a proliferation of authorities which inhabitants must endure. Thus in July 1982, popularly elected councils at the level of *Collectivité*, the zone and the region were established in Kivu [*Newbury, 1984a*]. In 1988, MPR 'MOPAP' representatives at the *Groupement* level were appointed. In 1988, new *Cités* were created and new chiefs installed in them. In 1989, Kivu was divided into three regions. North Kivu, previously a sub-region, became a region and new administrative personnel and infrastructure had to be built. To raise revenues, new taxes have been introduced and old ones increased, especially at the level of the *Collectivité* in the rural areas, and at the zone and sub-region levels in urban areas.

Decentralisation has devolved further power onto those exercising authority in rural areas: the feudal chiefs, wealthy businessmen, plantation owners, soldiers and to a lesser extent, wealthy villagers. As has historically been the case, once plantation owners, traditional chiefs and the military acquire greater autonomy and forge alliances among themselves (and also now with state politicians), unprotected cultivators suffer more insecure land rights and reduced freedom of labour. As Newbury has documented: 'State and local authorities collaborated in forcing residents off their land and providing labour and other resources, in return for certain services and other prerogatives from the plantation companies' [*Newbury, 1986: 102*]. Hired military harassment, 'arrests, extortion, and crop destruction are used against farmers who refused to abandon homes and fields coveted by those in power' [*Schoepf and Schoepf, 1988: 111*].

To sum up, then, although planners might consider road building to be synonymous with development, the concrete situation prevailing in the Zairian countryside during this period of crisis and adjustment implies that as the landscape is 'developed' by building roads, and as agriculture (ranching) is made more profitable, the developed landscape and its developed economy is unfortunately appropriated.

THE MARKET, THE ROADS AND FOOD SECURITY

Issues of direct expropriation of land, labour and money do not satisfactorily account for the differing opinions and factions over the road question. Attitudes are influenced by certain current and deeply felt social changes associated with roads. In particular these concern the way that roads affect the relationship between spouses within households (*urugo*). Women and men can use roads and marketing as resources in their struggle to maintain or improve their respective economic status in increasingly impoverished households. As they do so, however, their actions contribute to changing the way work is organised in the household and in the village; and this in turn affects the entire farming system, which has important implications for food security.

Food security used to be an aspect of general security which depended on membership in one of the 100 or so large patrikin communities (*umuryango*) in Bwisha. Every aspect of past food provisioning (cultivation, storage, eating, gifts and exchanges) invoked social allegiances and duties. Cultivating together in large groups (*guguzanya*), as well as the existence of formal (tribute) and informal transfers of food and labour, were the essence of alliance and community.

The community nature of food security is exemplified by the organisation of work groups. Although land for seasonal crops was allocated to each household, cultivation involved large, gender specific work groups which cultivated the plot of each household in turn. Participants in women's groups received gifts of a basket of food each day, and at harvest women received a large basket of millet from those who had not reciprocated their labour. Villagers with poor yields had little difficulty in acquiring food.

Food could be solicited in times of shortage from one's network of interdependents, which might include relatives, trading partners and friends. Persistent food transfers among these groups reinforced the relationship. Surpluses and shortages in different households were balanced through informal gift giving and reciprocity, more in terms of friendship, perhaps, than along strict kinship lines, but usually among relatives never-theless.

Networks of interdependents span the highly diversified agro-ecological regions of Bwisha. Farmers alter their crops, timing and techniques according to the different climatic conditions and land availability found over a wide range of altitudes. In densely populated regions of high altitude on the Rift Valley escarpment, or on the foothills of the volcanoes (from 1,800–2,800m), farming is conditioned by low temperatures and long rainy seasons (around 2,500mm of rain per year) and by land scarcity. In contrast, on the less densely populated base of the Rift Valley at less than 1,000m, farmers adapt to high temperatures and short, distinct rainy seasons (with around 1,000mm of rain per year).

Different crops and varieties are of course suited to particular altitudes. At higher altitudes farmers grow sorghum, beans, potatoes, maize and peas whereas at lower altitudes they cultivate bananas, cassava, millet, beans, maize, peanuts and coffee. Thus during the two altitude-specific cultivation seasons, when low food stocks coincide with high labour demands, nearby regions at other altitudes have abundant food, and social links have traditionally been used to solicit food from interdependents there. If a seasonal failure of the crop affected one region, food could also be obtained from other regions which were not so affected.

Food security and the benefits of complementarity were therefore assured mainly within large communities and social networks which linked peoples of different ethnic groups, occupations and agro-ecological areas. Spreading one's network duties and responsibilities far and wide was advantageous, and alliances with distant communities through marriage and blood pacts (*ukunyana*) were frequent.

Prudent leaders also stored millet and sorghum as famine reserves. Millet stores almost indefinitely, and sorghum lasts about two years. Through the tribute and taxation system, local and regional chiefs could build up strategic stocks which they could then use to their advantage during times of hunger. Although surplus food production usually had no value except as gifts, in times of famine it could even be exchanged for cattle, or used to attract dependent labourers. Dangerous, temporary markets formed during famines.

Except for such times of scarcity, these non-capitalist forms of production and exchange generally underwrote not only the food consumption of villagers, but also of workers on the plantations and in the mines. Plantation workers did not purchase food but were fed by their families; and to feed the mineworkers, farmers in their locality (although not in Bwisha) were compelled to deliver non-commercialised surpluses. Thus the plantation system left 'no base for an African rural petty capitalism nor for an African peasant agriculture' [*Peemans, 1986: 72*].

The system of collective responsibility for food security just described has crumbled under the impact of a number of changes, including a very high level of population growth. Between 1929 and 1986, the population of Bwisha rose from 63,000 to 263,000, implying a shift in the ratio of inhabitants per hectare of land from 46 to 192. Land shortages are now very acute in the highlands and the traditional system of land lending, through structures of clientelism outside the boundaries of the market, has broken down. Land has become a commodity which can be bought and sold, and land is rented at commercial rates. In Bwisha, the 47 per cent of all village households without sufficient land to sustain themselves in areas of traditional jurisdiction have no choice but to farm in the derelict plantations at the cost of a man-day of *corvée* per week. Patrilineal communities have fragmented.

A market for food developed in tandem with these agrarian changes, and as an outgrowth of related developments within the labour market. The sale of food was apparently insignificant in Bwisha until the 1950s [*Drevet, 1977*], when the abolition of unfree labour arrangements created some limited monetary demand for food products. This process gathered considerable momentum during the following decade, however, as food markets developed spontaneously in the deregulatory and chaotic aftermath of independence, when prices skyrocketed in expanding urban centers. The economic crisis of the past two decades has further drawn rural households into the market. Opportunities to migrate or engage in nearby wage labour have declined and it has become necessary to sell household crops in order to obtain cash, even when production should be consumed by the household itself.

Thus food security now depends more on using the market well than on creating alliances well. Buying food in the market, trading for profit, and day labour (often in other ecological zones) have become important strategies for meeting personal food deficits. At the same time, the tendency to withhold gifts and keep potentially profitable stores private during periods of hardship (in spite its moral wrongness), although not new, is spreading. Women of poor families cannot meet the food requests of friends and their 'obligations' to relatives. Those well-off women who can do so find that their support networks have shrunk because migration and land commoditisation has fragmented kin-based residential communities. The 'community' as constructed in (and dependent for its existence on) food gifts and land loans has become limited to the close family and perhaps the few other relatives, church-goers, and neighbours with whom good relations are maintained. Gifts are harder to solicit and are considered in terms of exact (value) reciprocity.

Such trends are viewed with anxiety by the people of Bwisha. Good 'community relations' are locally contrasted with bad 'market' ones. For many, the need to procure food from the market, especially soon after harvest, still indicates a 'lack of community' and earns disrespect. (The ideal of 'not having to buy food' should, however, not be confused with 'self-sufficiency'. The ideal is premised on upholding community relations, not on the risk averse and secure food provisioning strategy of any single 'co-operative household unity'.) The competition between family members for diminishing household resources is so great that households which have such common purpose are now hard to maintain.

CONFLICTS OF INTEREST IN HOUSEHOLDS, AND THEIR RESOLUTION

From the 1970s onward, the growing importance of the market for food crops and decline in the social value of non-market food exchanges have created confusion within households over the rights of different members to sell or otherwise control the use of these crops. Ambiguities arise in particular because men may consider that they control household wealth (which in earlier times did not encompass food, since food was not marketed), whereas women have always considered the disposal of food crops as their concern. This ongoing and unresolved conflict is covered up when household relations are harmonious, as due consideration is paid by each spouse to the other; but it becomes apparent whenever relations deteriorate, and most especially when supplies are running short.

Ambiguities in control over harvests are worse in certain circumstances. First, if food is stored in the house, because problems of rights to it become problems of storage itself. Second, if crop production requires a consider-able input from men, since men are more inclined to consider food crops which they helped to cultivate as theirs. Third, if the harvests are bulky and valuable, since men consider bulk stores of seasonal produce as under their control. Large stores also tempt husbands to reduce the financial assistance they provide to wives for the purchase of items such as clothes.

Under such circumstances, many (especially poorer) women engage in strategies to avoid losing control. They cultivate crops which men participate less in producing, they cultivate out of seasonal patterns to limit bulk supply, and they sell stocks earlier.

Crops with Less Participation on the Part of Men

Women cannot easily sell the major crops, such as millet, sorghum and climbing beans, which men help them to produce; but it is harder for men to dispute their wives' exclusive rights to any inter-crops they plant. Thus, for example, while women may not control millet (the household crop par excellence), they do control its inter-crops (for example, sorghum). The new food crops (cassava, bush beans, soja and colocasia) which have been adopted since the mid-1970s, and which now predominate for many households in Bwisha, were in fact all introduced by women as inter-crops.

Women plant cassava wherever they can get away with it, inter-cropped with millet, peanuts, bush beans, soja and coffee, or on its own in an exhausted field. They plant colocasia in coffee groves, on the fringe of banana groves, and on odd plots near the house. In Bwisha, as Guyer [*1986: 100*] has argued elsewhere, field and inter-cropping types which women control have become the backbone of the food system, whereas crops which men help produce have greatly diminished in importance.

Aseasonal Production

Women now sow seasonal crops such as beans and maize over longer periods; and making use of varieties of variable precocity, they harvest them over even longer spans of time. Seasons are less demarcated, harvest periods are longer, and storage is reduced. Storage is more 'in the field' than in the house.

The trend toward aseasonal crop production (and thus toward women's control over food cropping) is accentuated because intensive agriculture, inter-cropping and modern labour relations favour both the production of such aseasonal root crops as sweet potatoes and cassava, and the creative use of crop varieties and associations which break with old seasonal timings.

Selling

Women find it easier to store money than food, as money can be stored secretly, perhaps in women's savings groups (*ikibina*) where cash is secure from other claimants. Money can then be used as working capital for trading. By selling 'too much', women can also manage crises. During periods of difficulty, husbands are responsible for making up shortfalls of food or seed; and women can use this reversal of household obligations to force men to provide more for the family. In consequence, the increased use of the market in food provisioning seems not merely to be an outgrowth of land shortage and poverty, but to be accentuated by the struggle over rights to household produce.

Market integration is further exaggerated by very large price variations which tempt cultivators to speculate with their food stores. A higher proportion of food reaching the market, a greater reliance on purchases from it, and more long-distance traders who bring external influences to local markets, all magnify price fluctuations. In January 1987, the price of beans was Z 600 per sack; by July 1987 it had climbed more than tenfold to Z 7,200, and then by December, it had fallen to Z 2,400. In 1988, beans were at Z 2,500 per sack in June, but by December 1988 they had gone up four fold to Z 10,000. In 1989, things were different: in June 1989, a sack cost Z 21,000 but by November the price had halved to Z 10,000.

The potential for such huge price changes makes the gains or losses from speculation tremendous. No one can avoid being a speculator: one becomes a speculator even by default. Therefore, correct market decisions have become as important as correct production ones. And the inescapable necessity to 'play the market' strongly influences the provisioning strategies of households.

While there used to be a division of household labour *within* the production of unmarketed 'household' crops (millet, sorghum and climbing beans), the tendency as shown above is now for labour to be divided *between* crops which can be sold for cash: women concentrate on certain new crops, and men concentrate on others, including bananas and coffee. Old 'household' crops have as a result become marginalised.

This tendency is somewhat mitigated, however, by other arrangements which can be made to allocate communally cultivated crops individually while removing the ambiguity inherent in joint productive activities. For example, a field can be allocated to an individual (man or woman) who grows private crops (any crop, be it old or new, normally men's or normally women's) for his or her own unambiguous financial benefit (*kwihalika*). Such arrangements were previously made only for boys, but they are now made between spouses.

To accommodate the gender division of labour between spouses (or unmarried men and women) who are embarking on private production, reciprocal arrangements are made of the nature: 'if *you* (man) clear *my* (woman) bean field then *I* (woman) will sow *your* beans or weed *your* coffee,

or buy *you* some beers, or give *you* some money at harvest.' Such arrangements are understood between (and so instantiate the presence of)
economic 'individuals', and they occur at every stage of production and
consumption. In polite society these arrangements are disapproved of:
kwikora (to work for oneself) is considered *kwireba* (to be selfish). To avoid
this, some families overcome conflicts of interest over ambiguously controlled crops by allocating harvests to projects (food, school fees, women's
clothes, a bicycle, a tax, bridewealth) before cultivation, rather than leaving
their use ambiguous or earmarking them anti-socially for individuals.

The new individualism and reliance on the market have major dietary
implications. Greater use of aseasonal and associated crops means that
cassava and maize have largely replaced millet. Earlier selling implies that
the diet is downgraded to hunger season foods earlier, and that many people
rely on day labour, food purchase and other coping strategies earlier in the
hungry season. Changes in the marketing and consumption of beans testify
to this. They are increasingly a luxury which poorer people eat in quantity
only at harvest time. In general, they are sold; and the proceeds are used to
buy low-value bulk foods like cassava. Concomitantly, farmers choose
varieties which sell better, rather than those which 'taste good' or which are
better suited agro-ecologically.

As households have less local control over their diet, the latter also varies
more throughout the year, because of seasonal fluctuations in food prices
and seasonal differences in the purchasing power of farmers. Integration
into the market renders poor villagers very vulnerable to large price
increases, like those which occurred in 1989, when the price of basic staple
foods (cassava and maize) rose to 700 per cent of the level prevailing during
previous years. On that occasion, famine threatened Bwisha.

MARKETS, ROADS AND SOCIAL CHANGE

It should now be clear how diets and food provisioning strategies indicate to
Banyabwisha certain forms of economic and social relations in the household and community. Diet is at the centre of personal, class and ethnic
identities, all of which are changing rapidly. Some groups and individuals
are gaining, but most are losing, as market incorporation proceeds. And
even in the case of those who are able to devise new strategies for defending
their interests, gains are won at a price: those women who see that the road
might help them both to 'get by' and to battle for their economic rights in the
household, but who also see that it might exacerbate the reasons for that
battle, have realised the intractability of their situation.

Do the standard prescriptions of adjustment-related food policy have any
relevance to basic livelihood dilemmas in a region like Bwisha? Agreement

between the national government and international creditors to limit the role of the state in marketing, and to increase producer prices, is obviously irrelevant in the context of the market for agricultural products of the kind just discussed. Prices are being determined in a highly fragmented and circumscribed market, still in the process of development. Women sell food produce and men sell coffee in weekly markets by the road, where local purchasers compete with traders who come on foot from other regions or who have lorries. The state plays no part in this, except to the extent that public officials form part of the group of local power-holders who levy fines and collect bribes in the markets and on the roads. This is as much an example of private initiative as of public policy.

Developing a better network of roads can of course in principle serve to integrate the fragmented market and to smooth out the enormous variation in prices for food products which currently threatens the livelihood of the poor in areas like Bwisha. Roads in themselves, however, are not the issue. Their impact depends upon who controls them; and the situation described above is congruent with a violent and monopolistic form of market intervention, not one which fosters impartial competition.

The livelihood of most people in Bwisha is currently very precarious, for a variety of reasons having to do not only with the broader economic crisis, but also with climatic disturbances, epidemic diseases of cassava, the growing nightmare of AIDS, the collapse of coffee prices, erosion and declining soil fertility, as well as social disorganisation and the collapse of collective mechanisms of support. Village land is being expropriated as a concomitant of the expansion of cattle ranching, which rural development programmes tend to encourage. The number of landless is growing. Imposition of requirements to provide free labour services ensures that many people work part of the time for nothing; and even when they work for wages, the real level of remuneration for their labour is declining. Extortion, corruption and taxes are on the rise. The problem of survival in Bwisha is complex indeed, and the view from above is extraordinarily simple.

NOTES

1. Unless otherwise referenced, data on Zaire's debt situation is taken from Leslie's comprehensive analysis of the relationship of Zaire with the IMF and World Bank [*Leslie, 1987*].
2. Throughout this article, fictitious names have been used to identify field sites.

REFERENCES

Anstey, R., 1966, *King Leopold's Legacy*, London: Oxford University Press.

Callaghy, T., 1986, 'The International Community and Zaire's Debt Crisis', in Nzongola-Ntalaja (ed.), *The Crisis in Zaire: Myths and Realities*, Trenton, NJ: Africa World Press.

Drevet, J.F., 1977, 'Les plantations européenes dans le Kivu d'altitude', unpublished doctoral thesis in geography, Paris: Université de Paris X.

Dupriez, H., 1987, 'Bushi, l'asphyxie d'un peuple', unpublished manuscript.

Guyer, J.I., 1986, 'Intra-Household Processes and Farming Systems Research: Perspectives from Anthropology', in J.L. Moock (ed.), *Understanding Africa's Rural Households and Farming Systems*, Boulder, CO and London: Westview Press.

Kabongo, I., 1986, 'Myths and Realities of the Zairian Crisis', in Nzongola-Ntalaja (ed.), *The Crisis in Zaire: Myths and Realities*, Trenton, NJ: Africa World Press.

Katuala Kaba-Kashala and Mwamba Tshibasu, 1986, 'Les grands conflicts fonciers de Nord-Kivu. Philosophie, action préventive et rectificative', Rapport de la Commission Foncière Sous-Régionale de Nord-Kivu, Mouvement Populaire de la Révolution, Goma.

Kawata, B., 1989, 'L'endettement extérieur du Zaire', *Afrique* (Zaire), No.227, Sept., pp.351–70.

Leslie, W.J., 1987, *The World Bank and Structural Transformation in Developing Countries: The Case of Zaire*, Boulder, CO and London: Lynne Reinner.

MacGaffey, J., 1987, *Entrepreneurs and Parasites: The Struggle for Indigenous Capitalism in Zaire*, Cambridge: Cambridge University Press.

Mendiaux, E., 1956, 'Le Comité National du Kivu', *Revue Congolaise* (Zaire), Oct., pp.803–13 and Nov., pp.927–64.

Newbury, C., 1984a, 'Dead and Buried or Just Underground? The Privatization of the State in Zaire', *Canadian Journal of African Studies*, Vol.18, No.1, pp.112–14.

Newbury, C., 1984b, 'Ebutumwa bw'emihogo: The Tyranny of Cassava: A Women's Tax Revolt in Eastern Zaire', *Canadian Journal of African Studies*, Vol.18, No.1, pp.35–54.

Newbury, C., 1986, 'Survival Strategies in Rural Zaire: Realities of Coping with Crisis', in Nzongola-Ntalaja (ed.), *The Crisis in Zaire: Myths and Realities*, Trenton, NJ: Africa World Press.

Northrup, D., 1988, *Beyond the Bend in the River: African Labor in Eastern Zaire, 1865–1940*, Ohio: Ohio University Monographs in International Studies, Africa Series, No.52.

Nzabandora Ndi Mubanzi, 1984, 'Les expropriations foncières effectuées au Projet du P.N.A. et les réactions des paysans au Nord-Kivu (Zaire): 1925–1981', *Cahiers de CERPRU, (Revue du Centre d'Etudes et de Recherches pour la Promotion Rurale, ISDR Bukavu)*, No.1, pp.41–98.

Onimode, Bade, 1987, 'The IMF, World Bank and Africa', Report of the conference: 'The Impact of IMF–World Bank Policies on the People of Africa' convened by the Institute for African Alternatives, City University, London, 7–10 Sept. 1987.

Peemans, J.P., 1986, 'Accumulation and Underdevelopment in Zaire: General Aspects in Relation to the Evolution of the Agrarian Crisis', in Nzongola-Ntalaja (ed.), *The Crisis in Zaire: Myths and Realities*. Trenton, NJ: Africa World Press.

Schatzberg, M.G., 1988, *The Dialectics of Oppression in Zaire*, Bloomington, IN: Indiana University Press.

Schoepf, B.G. and C. Schoepf, 1987, 'Food Crisis and Agrarian Change in the Eastern Highlands of Zaire', *Urban Anthropology*, Vol.16, No.1, pp.5–37.

Schoepf, B.G. and C. Schoepf, 1988, 'Land, Gender and Food Security in Eastern Kivu, Zaire', in J. Davison, *Agriculture, Women and Land: The African Experience*, Boulder, CO and London: Westview Press.

Thomas, S., and M. Reintsma, 1989, 'Zaire's Economic Liberalization and Its Impact in the Agricultural Sector', *Development Policy Review*, Vol.7, No.1, pp.29–50.

The Finance of Trade and Agriculture in a Backward Area of Bangladesh

BEN CROW and K.A.S. MURSHID

Over large areas of the rural Third World, markets for land, labour, credit and goods are interlocked, so that the terms of exchange established in one area (for example, access to credit) affect those prevailing in another (such as the price at which grain can be sold). The implications for rural livelihood and government policy of arrangements of this kind are analysed below, with reference to a backward paddy-producing area of Bangladesh.

This article is concerned with the finance of trade and agriculture in a backward area of Bangladesh. It indicates that there is a strong case for market reform, but the price- and state-focused reforms of the 1980s have had little influence on the markets of the area. The dominance of absentee landlords and moneylending merchants, and their provision of expensive and restrictive credit, have not been affected by the reduction of state involvement in agricultural markets.

The article describes the unusual forms of financial relation those dominant groups have used to constitute a hierarchy of interlocked market relationships. It indicates how (i) cash loans from traders to poor peasants secured against the harvest (and fixing its price) and (ii) loans tying small traders to large brokers establish the connections in a hierarchy of intermediaries which dominates agricultural trade and finance in the area. The stability of this hierarchy appears to derive from the ability of a dominant group of brokers and absentee landlords to control (a) transport, (b) the provision of security, (c) the supply of credit, and (d) key elements of the information required for trade.

This hierarchy of intermediaries with its associated financial contracts has not been found in an area of advanced agriculture. There, higher levels of

Ben Crow, Food Research Institute, Stanford University; K.A.S. Murshid, Bangladesh Institute of Development Studies. The findings reported in this article come from a joint research project of the British Open University and the Bangladesh Institute of Development Studies, funded by the Overseas Development Administration of the United Kingdom. The article rests primarily on the detailed research of Tarit Datta Gupta and Shahid ur Rashid.

agricultural investment, the adoption of green revolution technologies and higher yields and cropping intensities are associated with a greater separation of markets for land, labour, money and commodities.

The article has implications both for analysis and for policy. For analysis, it re-emphasises the importance of the wider social context in the understanding of interlocked market relations and suggests some of the dynamics of change within the sphere of commerce. For policy, the study suggests that there are serious limitations to the efficacy of price-based food policies.

MARKET REFORM AND THE PROBLEM OF INTERLOCKED MARKETS IN BANGLADESH

At independence in 1971, Bangladesh inherited a public food distribution system first established by the British government of India in the 1940s and continued by the government of Pakistan between 1947 and 1971. The system was primarily designed to ensure the food supply of large urban populations. It concentrated the efforts of the state, through its Food Department, on the procurement of large quantities of grain and the subsequent distribution of that grain to selected urban groups at subsidized prices. During the 1960s and early 1970s, local procurement was gradually overtaken by food aid as the principal source of grain for the public distribution system; and the political sensitivity of food prices also encouraged an increasing level of subsidy in the ration price. Together, these changes contributed to the growth of an indefensible government position in foodgrain markets. Significant proportions of government expenditure (financed primarily through food aid) were being devoted to the provision of cheap food to relatively better-off groups in the urban population.

At an earlier point than in many developing countries, aid donors and the government of Bangladesh began to consider the need for reform of this urban provisioning structure [*Crow, 1990*]. In 1976, a group of USAID economists put together an agenda of reforms reflecting concern about food insecurity and the high cost of government involvement in foodgrain markets. Five main changes were proposed:

  (i) greater reliance on private foodgrain markets;
 (ii) reduction of the public food distribution system;
(iii) elimination of subsidised food distribution to urban populations;
 (iv) introduction of a scheme of open market sales and price stabilisation; and
  (v) generally higher food prices.

These proposals were not strongly resisted by the government, which implemented the main principles of the reform during the 1980s. The proportion of food distributed by the private sector has increased, the subsidy on grain distributed by the public sector has been reduced and the proportion of publicly distributed grain going to better-off groups is now far lower than in the 1970s or early 1980s. The share of food subsidy in government expenditure was reduced from a peak of 9.5 per cent in 1982 to one per cent in 1987 [*World Bank, 1988: Table 2.5*].

Such reforms improved the macroeconomic position of the government of Bangladesh, but they overlooked serious problems of grain markets in rural areas of the country, where an extremely complex structure of private trade conditions the livelihood of the mass of the population.

Studies of grain markets in Bangladesh therefore merit close attention and have important implications for policy.[1] One kind of rural exchange environment, to be discussed here, rests on a system of particularly exploitative social relations, implying obvious need for reform. This is the structure of interlocked markets which can be found in backward areas of the country, and indeed in backward areas of many other parts of the world.

The concept of interlocked markets refers to the contractual tying of the terms of exchange in two sets of transactions [*Ellis, 1988: 150*]. Entry into the first 'market' (land leasing, for example) establishes the terms of participation in a second 'market' (with labour or output being provided at less than prevailing rates to the landowner). Sharecropping is one example of market interlocking, where the provision of land permits its owner to establish conditions for the tenants' payment, in output and/or in labour. Others, described in this study, involve loans extended by merchants to poor peasants, who must in turn supply crops on set terms to the lender; or provision of working capital by large merchants to small ones, in order to tie the latter to the former throughout a trading season (or longer).

Bhaduri [*1986*] describes how interlocked markets can lie behind a process of forced commercialisation, in which peasant households become involuntary participants in the market, selling goods which should be kept for family subsistence or delivering them on terms which are highly disadvantageous. The establishment and reproduction of such a regime depends to a considerable extent on the political dominance of rentier landlords, moneylenders and merchants in the ruling order [*Bhaduri, 1981*] and ultimately on the slow pace of development of alternative employment opportunities [*Bharadwaj, 1985*]. The maintenance of technological backwardness and poverty among peasant households constitutes a central element in the model, since innovation introduces the possibility that subordinated households can accumulate money and gain independence.

As Srivastava [*1989: 496*] has pointed out, however, the longer-term evolution of interlocked market relations depends on the peculiarities of specific local, regional and national contexts, and 'may be consistent with precapitalist relations and strategies, or with the creation of requirements for emergent capitalism, or simultaneously contain "contradictory" features of both aspects'. Those who appropriate the resources of their dependents within the commercial structure of these backward, exploitative markets can make many uses of their capital. It follows that study of the wider contemporary and historical context within which interlinked markets arise may be more revealing than abstract modelling of the formal features of relations between individuals.

INTRODUCTION TO THE BACKWARD AREA

The backward area we have studied is in southern Bangladesh, in the district of Noakhali. We have concentrated on two large foodgrain markets collecting paddy and distributing rice, two local village markets within the hinterland of each of the collection markets, and a sample of 100 rural households selected from the areas served by the village markets.

One of the collection markets studied acts as an important import and export market for a large area of Noakhali. Its immediate hinterland is a relatively backward single cropped area in which productivity of the land is low and investment in new agricultural technology slight. We will refer to this market only as it enters into competition with a second grain collecting centre, in a 'frontier' region, on which detailed attention will be focussed in this article.

Some 18 miles from the import–export market, there is an area of *char* land, or land newly formed by riverine action, which is predominantly single cropped, with paddy cultivation during the *Aman* season (from August to November) constituting the main agricultural activity.

The historical sequence of settlement in this region, one which is not untypical of *char* and island areas of Bangladesh, established sharecropping under the control of absentee landlords. When the land was submerged in the 1950s by riverine action, the original landowners migrated to other parts of the country. Separated from their means of livelihood, many of them were immiserated. The land was then reclaimed through the construction of a cross dam, or large earth embankment, in the mid-1960s. Some of the original residents were able to reclaim their property, but a process of land-grabbing ensured that the major share of the land went to new owners, those who had most power to push (mostly false) claims through the courts and most muscle to fight land-grabbing battles. The latter installed new migrants as sharecropper tenants on their land, while they became or remained resident in the nearby towns.

Within the *char* area, land productivity is low. This is only partly because opportunities for the expansion of tubewells, prefiguring growth in other parts of the country, are limited (in the absence of large scale development of polders) by the potential for saline water incursion. The more fundamental reason is that the investment and collective action necessary to create effective water control are actively opposed by the local ruling order.[2]

Despite low yields and little apparent district wide surplus [*Giasuddin and Hamid, 1986*], there are sizeable exports of paddy from the *char* area in the months after the harvest, and imports of rice back to the *char* area in the remaining six to eight months of the year. Since the land was created in the 1960s, there has in fact been a rapid expansion of traders and village market places to procure the paddy crop and distribute rice to consumers. This has inevitably entailed an expansion of trading capital.

CREDIT HIERARCHY, TRADE CIRCUITS AND TYPES OF CREDIT RELATION

The large *char* area grain collection market stands at the apex of a hierarchy of financial relationships which channel cheap paddy from the *char* area to moneylending traders and absentee landlords. This hierarchy, depicted in Figure 1, can be seen as having two functions. During the post-harvest trading season, it secures the supply of paddy to the traders at its apex. In the lean months (for both peasant consumption and trading) when the crop is growing, it provides circuits for investment of capital with high returns.

In Figure 1 and in the discussion here, we focus primarily on the way in which the hierarchy interlocks the credit and grain markets. It should nevertheless be noted that the hierarchy is wider than this. A large portion of grain goes directly to resident and absentee landlords under agreements which promise a share of the crop for the use of land. There are also agreements in which smallholders and tenants promise to pay in grain when they receive labour servicies, commodities or the use of equipment (notably milling and threshing equipment), but these account for a much smaller proportion of exchange. The hierarchy is thus a generalised interlocking of capital, land, output and labour markets, and the moneylending merchants are only one section of the social group at the apex of the hierarchy to benefit from the extraction of surplus product.

The structure of commercial power characteristic of the *char* area is maintained through control of local political structures and the police, the use of private thugs, and the existence of a transport cartel, established not long after the formation of the new *char* land by the local ruling order in the dominant market town. The cartel is enforced by a Truck Association, most of the members of which are merchants.

FIGURE 1

HIERARCHY COLLECTING PADDY FROM THE BACKWARD AREA

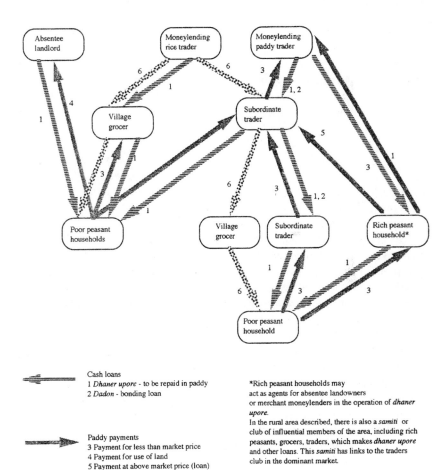

Cash loans
1 *Dhaner upore* - to be repaid in paddy
2 *Dadon* - bonding loan

Paddy payments
3 Payment for less than market price
4 Payment for use of land
5 Payment at above market price (loan)

Rice loans
6 at risk of usury
7 on favourable terms

*Rich peasant households may
act as agents for absentee landowners
or merchant moneylenders in the operation of *dhaner upore*.
In the rural area described, there is also a *samiti* or
club of influential members of the area, including rich
peasants, grocers, traders, which makes *dhaner upore*
and other loans. This *samiti* has links to the traders
club in the dominant market.

Trucks from other regions are not allowed to carry goods within the jurisdiction of the Association. They can bring goods into the *char* area, but they must leave empty and they are forbidden to transport cargo between two local destinations. The Association has defined its jurisdiction to include the hinterland of the market dominating the *char* area, as well as the local district headquarters town. This area includes the local government food-grain storage depot (LSD).

In order to sustain its monopoly, the Association has three employees known as 'linemen' who observe the movement of trucks from other areas. These linemen are paid a monthly salary of Tk 1,200–1,400 each (equivalent to the salary of a moderately paid government employee), and they are also able to receive payments from the drivers of the trucks. If trucks from other areas pass through the territory of the Association, they are stopped and fined.

The immediate monetary benefits of this cartel can be observed by comparing the Truck Association rates with those charged along similar routes outside its jurisdiction. Within the controlled area, Tk 5.50 carries 1 maund of paddy 15 miles; outside it, the same amount carries 1 maund of paddy 60 to 70 miles. Thus the Truck Association monopoly adds more than 400 per cent to the cost of carrying paddy.

This arrangement makes it very expensive for local traders without their own trucks to hire transport, it reinforces the exclusive nature of the small group of local merchants who control the grain trade, and it prevents competitors outside the region from operating in the *char* area. Thus it forms one element in the apparatus which protects an exploitative commercial hierarchy, complementing their control of insecurity as a way of segmenting the markets of this area.

Until a few years ago there was a comparable truck association operating with monopoly privileges in the nearby import-export market. It was broken with the help of local political leaders when a syndicate of drivers, some truck owners and traders formed a competing association which charged competitive rates. The truck association of the *char* area had more staying power because alternative routes into the *char* area are few and difficult (the town sits at the apex of roads serving the *char* area). No organised competition threatened this cartel during the period of the research. Since then, however, the cartel has been challenged and has begun to break down. It is testimony to the multivalent power of the moneylending traders that the failure of this barrier to entry has not apparently threatened the extraction hierarchy. Their ability to ensure physical and financial security (for themselves and their subordinates), to control credit and to have preferential access to trade information is adequate to maintain the dominance of this group in the markets of the area.

The flow of grain from the mass of poor peasant households to the apex of the local commercial structure is assured through two circuits of credit which tie both small producers and dependent paddy traders to moneylending merchants. The first of these, shown in Figure 1, involves a loan made by a trader, shopkeeper, rich peasant household, or absentee landlord to a poor peasant producer at the beginning of the agricultural season. This is a time when money is desperately needed by small cultivators to cover both costs of production and consumption. Known as *dhaner upore*, the loan is to be repaid with a part of the peasant's harvest, delivered to the lender at a price determined at the time the loan is made. In the case of *dhaner upore* credit extended to producers by small traders or village shopkeepers, the original source of the money is usually a large grain merchant, who provides resources to his subordinates and small-trading clientele at the outset of the growing season, for the specific purpose of on-lending to poor peasants as *dhaner upore*. *Dhaner upore* is the predominant form of credit for the majority of cultivators in the backward *char* area.[3]

The second credit relationship, called *dadon*, is a commercial transaction between a larger trader and a smaller one, in which there is no financing of production. It consists of a loan of working capital, made by large money-lending merchants to their subordinates, which permits local grain traders to finance their purchases from producers at harvest time. Through this mechanism, subordinate traders are bound to a specific moneylending merchant, delivering regular quantities of paddy to the latter. The frequency of these deliveries varies throughout the season (with peak frequencies when market supplies are plentiful, after the harvest), but the usual lapse of time between deliveries seems to be in the range of two to 15 days. There is a measure of compulsion for the subordinate trader to keep operating: the larger moneylending merchant may ask for his money to be returned if he feels that the borrower has not been supplying paddy with a regularity appropriate to the season and the operations of comparable traders in the market.

Although a *dadon* loan provides an amount of working capital which may not cover the cost of all operations of the subordinate trader, the latter agrees, when taking the loan, to supply all the paddy he gathers to the moneylending merchant. The *dadon*-giver is thus the recipient of a quantity of paddy with a value well in excess of (and often double) the amount of his loan.

Dadon is the principal way small traders obtain working capital in this area, but untied cash loans to traders are also available from local money-lenders and big cultivators, at a nominal interest rate of ten per cent per month. In addition, there has been some recent disbursement of funds through the Krishi (agricultural) bank; but its loans are small in number relative to demand, and those obtaining credit are mostly larger farmers and better-off local traders.

Three other forms of credit are associated with foodgrain transactions in the *char* area. Some surplus cultivators lend paddy to local traders. And at the other end of the social scale, some of the poorest groups use their savings to make loans, which are repayable in cash at the moneylending rate of ten per cent per month. Known as *jolati* loans, the latter seem to form part of emerging survival strategies of poor women [*Kabir, 1990*]. Finally, village grocery shops lend rice to poor peasants and labourers.

Figures 2(a) and 2(b) illustrate how the principal trading circuits of the *char* area operate in two different seasons of the year. In the three to four months after the *Aman* harvest of November–December, large flows of paddy leave the *char* area under the compulsions of sharecropping contracts, the need to repay loans and other forms of distress sale. Then, as the stocks of poor peasants are exhausted, the direction of flow is reversed and rice returns to the area, through the circuits shown in Figure 2(b), to feed local people during the lean months from March through October–November.

TRADER TYPES AND TRADER RELATIONS

Let us look more closely now at the principal actors in the interlocked market for credit and grain, and at the way they are interrelated.

Merchant Moneylender or Aratdar

There are about a dozen merchant moneylenders who have established themselves as the dominant suppliers of finance to agriculture and trade in the *char* area and, with absentee landlords, as the main recipients of paddy produced there. They describe themselves as brokers, middlemen between small traders collecting the paddy from the growers, on the one hand, and the longer distance traders taking it on to larger urban centres. Although they do fulfil this function, the moneylending merchants are distinguished from a larger number of 'free' brokers operating in the wholesale market, who carry out the same intermediary function but insist that they do not have *dhaner upore* and advance purchase relations with cultivators.

All commercial operations in the region are subject to a degree of confidentiality, but moneylending traders are more secretive than their 'free' counterparts because *dhaner upore* relations are socially unacceptable. Free traders are able to list those who undertake *dhaner upore* operations, and this list can be confirmed with the subordinates of the

FIGURE 2(A)

TRADE CIRCUIT IN BACKWARD AREA AFTER MAIN HARVEST

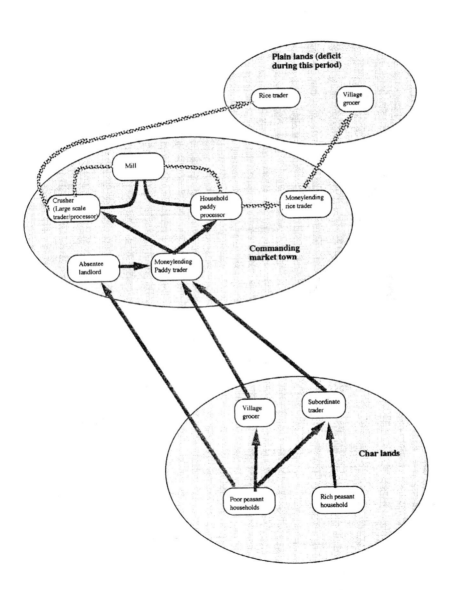

FIGURE 2(B)
TRADE CIRCUIT IN BACKWARD AREA AFTER BORO HARVEST (I.E. DEFICIT PERIOD)

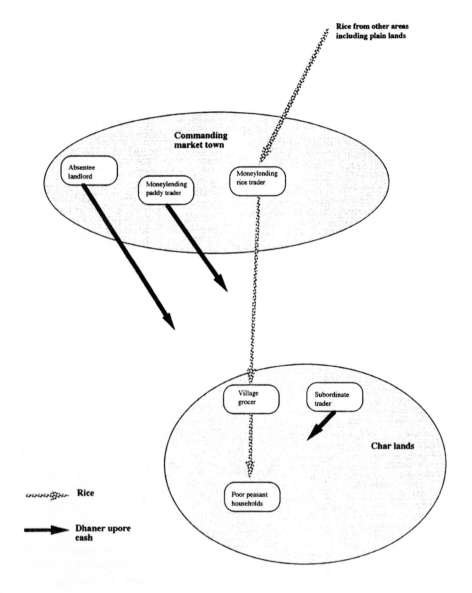

moneylending traders. Even the free traders have *dadon* relations, but the conditions of these relations are less restrictive and the proportion of their business operated through *dadon* is less than in the case of the moneylending trader.

Figure 3 describes the seasonal capital utilisation of one moneylending trader.[4] First, it indicates the timing of loans which he makes to his collection traders, for the purpose of on-lending to peasant producers as *dhaner upore*, or tied credit. Most of these loans have been disbursed by mid-July, which coincides with the end of land preparation and the beginning of transplanting for many *char* area cultivators. It is also a period of high prices when the stocks of grain of many households are exhausted and they are forced to purchase rice to sustain their consumption.

The trader-to-trader loans which underpin *dhaner upore* loans to cultivators have to be repaid to the moneylender by subordinate paddy buyers within a short and relatively well-defined period, seven to fifteen days after the start of the Aman harvest. This repayment is time-bound because the moneylending trader needs to redirect or recirculate the same capital as *dadon* loans tying his procurement traders to him. If during the pre-harvest season his profits depend on extending low velocity, high yield credit, in the form of production credit or *dhaner uphore*, during the post-harvest trading season his returns depend not primarily on usury but on rapid turnover. Some of his deals will involve his own buying and selling where the margin varies, but most will be commission arrangements. On the latter, his returns are less dependent on the price than on the speed of circulation of his *dadon* capital.

Figure 3 indicates the scale and duration of *dadon* lending. Most of the *dadon* loans have been repaid by the beginning of February, when the initial post-harvest peak of sales has begun to fall off. It is noted by free traders that the moneylending traders dominate transactions during this first peak, while the free traders handle a larger proportion during the second peak, some two to three months later, when paddy is sold by cultivators able to wait until higher prices prevail.

Not all *dadon* loans are collected. As with other forms of tied financial relationships, some of the loans are left out throughout the season. This may happen if the moneylending trader wishes to keep the subordinate under obligation for the next season. Alternatively it may reflect either the inability of the subordinate trader to repay the loan or the willingness of the moneylending trader to fund some of the other activities of the subordinate.

The fourth form of capital indicated in Figure 3 is a more straightforward advance of working capital, known as *paikari baki* (meaning advance to purchasers). Traders of all kinds sell grain on credit to those who buy from them. Sometimes there are conditions attached to this credit, most usually

FIGURE 3

MONEYLENDING MERCHANT'S SEASON CAPITAL UTILISATION

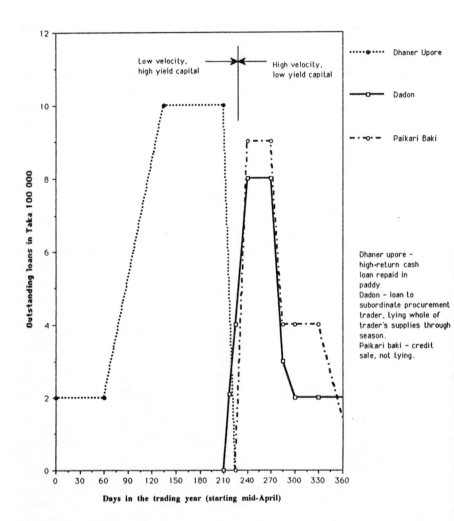

Days in the trading year (starting mid-April)

tying the purchaser to the *aratdar* for all his purchases; but in the case of the moneylending traders studied here, there seem to be no conditions. They provide a short-term loan of working capital which the purchaser pays back within a few days, probably on his next visit to that market. There is no explicit interest payment, but the taking of credit may be reflected in some price penalty.

Since the total amount of capital in use in this business varies on a seasonal basis, there are opportunities to divert resources to other enterprises during periods when there is a surplus of capital in the foodgrain trade. In fact, several of the merchant moneylenders of the region who have risen within the last 10 to 15 years to positions of great wealth and influence are now investing in other trades and businesses (selling building materials, establishing a hotel and a petrol station, among other activities). One of their number was chosen in 1989 by the Prime Minister to decide who should be government foodgrain dealers in the *char* area.

Subordinate Paddy Procurement Trader

Subordinate paddy collecting traders are numerous throughout the *char* areas and vary widely in their scale of operation. The smallest, often known as *farias*, may be operating with virtually no working capital, interspersing their trading activities with wage labour. These are among the poorest households of the area, with little economic stability or prospect of accumulation. At the other end of the scale, the bigger *beparis* may have Tk 2,000 to Tk 5,000 in working capital of their own and some potential for accumulation. Such traders tend to purchase or lease land. Whatever their size, virtually all these paddy buyers are tied to moneylending merchants in the dominant market town through financial arrangements which provide the bulk of their 'investment' and trading capital.

The ability of subordinate traders to make a living, and in some cases to accumulate sufficient resources to lessen their dependence on their patrons or to invest, depends upon their manipulation of the margin between the price they are able to fix with producers, when extending *dhaner upore* loans at planting time or simply when buying up grain after harvest, and the price paid them by large merchants when they deliver their grain to the central market, often under the restrictions imposed by a *dadon* relationship. The level of all of these prices obviously depends on the relative power of the parties involved, which produces an enormously complex range of outcomes. It is useful to review the evidence which is available on the way this process unfolds.

Table 1 provides data on the *dhaner upore* loans taken during the 1988 *Aman* season by 38 households (out of a sample of 50) in two villages in the backward *char* area of Noakhali. Two estimates are provided of the price loss which growers face through their use of this form of credit (and the consequent possibility for gain on the part of paddy procurement traders). The first compares the price the grower received for paddy pledged against a *dhaner upore* loan with the price that the same grower actually received for a non-tied sale at the homestead or in the market. This price is termed 'grower's loss one'.[5] The second comparison is made with the price that the moneylending merchant uses to value the paddy if the loan is rolled over into a second agricultural year. This price is equivalent to the price received by most absentee landlords when they sell their paddy.

One can conclude from this survey that dependent paddy traders are able, through the employment of *dhaner upore* loans, to create a margin between procurement and central market prices of between 25 and 50 per cent. How they actually fare in their business depends, however, on a number of factors, including the costs associated with risk-taking, transactions costs and – last but certainly not least – the ability of dependent traders to obtain a fair price from the merchant moneylenders to whom they ultimately sell the paddy they have procured.

The risks of *dhaner upore* are difficult to assess. Most subordinate traders do not keep consolidated accounts; and the books kept by traders are not available for detailed inspection.[6]

It is clear that the costs of outright default by growers, as well as the costs of the more usual delayed payment of *dhaner upore*, are largely borne by intermediaries, rather than by the moneylending merchants. Default rates do not, however, seem excessive. According to one estimate, five per cent of *dhaner upore* borrowers default; but small traders have effective institutional procedures for collecting their debts, with the help of their money-lending patrons, through the invocation of the *sailish* or village court. The *sailish* is made up of the most influential men of the area which, in the words of one intermediary, 'includes all of the *dhaner upore*-givers'. Small growers are allowed to attend the *sailish*, but they are not members; and as several traders commented, it is rare for the trader not to win his case: 'If the members of the *sailish* do not find a way to recover the amount, sometimes they force the grower to sell his bullock or other assets. In case they do not get the total amount, they try to get the cash amount invested with the grower.'

In the commanding market, the larger merchants do not emphasise their losses. One comments that he has never lost a loan in his business life. Another explains how he can force a defaulting grocery shop owner to sell his land in order to pay his obligations. A third says that he always wins his cases in the village *sailish* 'because members of the *sailish* have to come to this market and I have good connections with them'.

TABLE 1

GROWER LOSS AND TRADER RETURN FOR 104 DHANER UPORE LOANS

	Average	Range
VILLAGE 1		
Implicit DU price	138	117-166
Freesale price	209	190-222
Rollover price	253	250-260
Grower's price loss 1 (%)		25-45
Grower's price loss 2 (%)		34-54
Gross trader's return (%)	131	62-200
VILLAGE 2		
Implicit DU price	140	129-143
Freesale price	207	109-220
Rollover price	252	250-265
Grower's price loss 1 (%)		25-40
Grower's price loss 2 (%)		43-49

Notes: DU implicit price = loan/quantity of paddy paid. In the case of an agreement to pay 8 maunds per Tk 1,000, this is an implicit price of TK 125. (Prices are per kg maund, that is, a 'maund' of 40 kg)

Freesale price – price received by the grower for a sale (generally at the homestead) at the date nearest to the time when dhaner upore paddy was repaid (either a price within two or three days, or one interpolated between the nearest sales).

Rollover price – price at which the value of outstanding paddy debt is calculaed by the moneylending merchant. These prices are calculated from four cases where the debt was edtended in village 1 and seven cases in village 2.

The gross rates of return to *dhaner upore* also have to be viewed in the light of the costs of credit administration. For the merchant moneylenders these costs do not appear high. Since itinerant paddy traders routinely make regular deliveries of paddy to the warehouses of their patrons, large merchants do not have the costs in travel and time required for regular debt collection visits of the kind incurred by small traders in grain markets. In the realm of retail provisioning, rice traders do have to visit their networks of village shops in order to collect their debts. One of the largest rice traders estimates a monthly cost of Tk 300 to 400 for the collection of debt owed by the village shops and retailers he supplies. This is on a total circulating capital of Tk 300,000 to 400,000. It seems surprisingly cheap for so complex a hierarchy of credit relations.

The smaller the dependent paddy trader, the larger his margins must be in order to provide a semblance of livelihood for his family. Therefore, even if costs of administration and risk-taking do not eliminate the price advantage created by extending tied loans to producers, most traders are unlikely to accumulate capital. Their precarious position is compounded by their need to accept *dadon* loans from merchant moneylenders.

These supply-oriented loans of working capital not only tie the trader to a single moneylending merchant and transfer most of the risks of trade from the commission agent to the subordinate *dadon* trader, but also limit the capacity of the receiver to negotiate a sales price for the paddy he delivers. *Dadon* is generally provided as part of a commission or brokerage arrangement. The subordinate trader agrees to supply all of his procurement to the *dadon*-providing firm, and that firm agrees to sell the paddy at the market price, charging the subordinate trader (and the purchaser) a fixed commission related to the quantity of paddy sold.

In practice, the agreement is varied in two ways. The more solvent subordinate has some influence over the timing of the sale. In this case, the subordinate may request that the commission agent hold his stock until a specified market price is achieved. This first variation of the agreement is a simple function of the relative power of the two parties. An insignificant trader with no working capital can expect to have no influence over the timing of the sale of his paddy, whereas the more solvent and influential trader may get into arguments with the commission agent if he feels that his paddy would have achieved a better price had the sale been delayed by a day or two.

The second variation of the agreement concerns the dual role of the commission agent. Most commission agents, and all of the larger ones, combine brokerage with buying and selling on their own account. This allows them to extract the benefits of a rising market while avoiding the costs of a falling market and to do so in both overt and covert ways. When the *aratdar* expects the price to rise, he may simply inform his subordinate trader that a particular delivery is not a commission sale but a *kata dor* (fixed price) sale. In this way he can take the benefit of the price rise. But subordinate traders frequently complain that this transfer of the benefits of rising prices also occurs in covert ways: their *aratdar* may inform them that their delivery sold at one price, when they learn from other sources either that the price in the market was actually higher on the day he claimed to have sold their paddy, or that the paddy was not sold on the day that the *aratdar* reported.

Most subordinate traders are not in a position to pursue these claims with vigour. They depend for their livelihood upon the *dadon* loan provided by the *aratdar*. If they argue too vigorously, the *aratdar* can simply refuse to renew the loan. In addition to this direct economic subordination, the power and influence of the *aratdar* make him a forbidding adversary for a petty trader. Nevertheless, arguments do occur when subordinate traders achieve a degree of solvency.

Not all the risks of trade are transferred to the subordinate trader. The moneylending merchant can suffer a default on the part of dependent traders, particularly when crop output is exceptionally low due to flood, drought or other calamity. Traders giving *dadon* to subordinates who trade over long distances, such as the traders of Dhaka markets, also protect themselves against theft of their money by extending *dadon* only to traders they have come to trust, and initially extending only small amounts of capital. In the backward area of Noakhali, however, the generalised social control of the trading class acts as a constraint on default, as noted above in the case of *dhaner upore* loans. Unless the subordinate trader migrates, which does happen, the local *sailish* can seize assets or negotiate repayment arrangements for defaults on *dadon* obligations.

The Village Shop

It is at the village grocery shop that the full implications of distress sales by poor peasants, within a context of forced commerce, are revealed. Compelled by *dhaner upore* or pressing needs for cash to sell paddy at low prices for export out of the area, deficit producers eventually must meet consumption needs by purchasing rice (which may have been stored in the commanding market town or, more likely, is imported from the distress sales of another backward eastern region of the country).

The village grocery shop sells rice and other commodities at high prices, on credit which is apparently interest free. In fact, however, this credit involves a significant risk to the consumer, since default on his part may be transformed into an obligation to supply paddy on the same *dhaner upore* terms offered by the subordinate paddy procurement trader. There are thus penal debt arrangements threatening at both the production and consumption ends of the transactions of poor peasants.

The village shop is bound into the local provisioning hierarchy by three types of commodity–finance relationships. Supplies of rice and other commodities are taken on credit from moneylending merchants in the commanding market. This line of commodity credit contains the common bonding clause that the grocer cannot buy goods from another moneylending merchant without paying off his debts to the first. In this relationship there may be room for exceptions and negotiation, but the scope for default is not great. One shopkeeper had to sell some of his wife's gold to make full payment to his supplier. Another, who had suffered a series of thefts and calamities, was forced to supply one of his bullocks to his moneylending merchant in partial payment of his debt.

The grocer's second set of financial relations is analogous to the *dhaner upore* capital supplied to the subordinate paddy trader. As the lean season approaches its peak, the village grocer can seek cash from his commodity suppliers or other merchant and absentee moneylenders for investment with his consumers on *dhaner upore* terms. The grocer obtains these cash loans on terms paralleling those obtained by the subordinate trader: he enters into an obligation to repay the loan in paddy, but at a lower rate than he will charge to those who borrow from him.

Thirdly, the grocer lends commodities to the different categories of peasant in the *char* region, though not to those who are landless. He extends credit to more influential growers with larger amounts of land on preferential terms because they can do him a favour by lending him paddy during the high price period. These larger growers may need to borrow commodities at times of peak labour demand when they are feeding a large hired labour force. Their borrowing is essentially free.

To those who have less influence and economic standing, his credit may be more expensive. Rice and other commodities are available at the normal price, and no charge is made for credit provided the loan is repaid within a reasonable time, perhaps two or three weeks. There may be room for negotiation of the period if there is no agricultural work available at the time, and the peasant household therefore cannot earn the cash required for repayment. After a while, and as the lean season peaks, the grocer may become more insistent. At that point, the debt will frequently be transformed into a debt of paddy.

Like the subordinate paddy traders, there is considerable differentiation amongst the village shopkeepers. Some are accumulating and some are losing land and other assets. In general, however, the shopkeepers of this backward area appear to operate on a larger scale and play a more pivotal economic role than is the case in, for example, the non-*char* areas of

Noakhali (where the hierarchical commercial, tenurial and financial arrangements are not established to the degree evident in the *chars*).

Small Tied Paddy Processor

If the moneylending merchant (with the absentee landlord) is one of the commanding figures at the top of the hierarchy, the small paddy processor, or *bharkiwala*, is amongst those at the bottom of the pyramid. While the *bharkiwala* household may not be the poorest of those impoverished by the structure of backward agriculture, it is perhaps the most subordinated. The *bharkiwala* takes orders from three different captains of commerce – two of them moneylending merchants and the third a local miller, who may also advance loans to the processor.

Throughout most of Bangladesh, small-scale processing proceeds alongside larger-scale paddy parboiling and milling. Not more than 20 years ago, small-scale processors produced paddy from rice entirely through family labour, with the use of the *dheki*. Today, manual husking of paddy has largely been supplanted by the electric or diesel husking mill. *Bharkiwala* households (also known as *kutials* or cycle *beparis*, among other terms) now use family labour to soak, parboil and dry the paddy, and then go to the mills to remove the husk and bran.

It has been suggested [*Harriss, 1990*] in the case of India, and seems plausible for Bangladesh as well, that the fortunes of small-scale processing and trade may be critically dependent on the margins created by larger enterprises. Where large-scale trade has established a degree of oligopoly ensuring more profitable margins, economic space is created in which small processors may work. Their high costs and low labour productivity restrict their expansion in areas where trading and processing margins are squeezed, but they can operate in areas of oligopoly without representing a threat to large mills. (Frequently they serve local markets, while the large mills produce rice for long distance sale.) Nevertheless financial constraints, among other factors, make it virtually impossible for households engaged in such enterprises to ensure themselves more than a bare subsistence living.

Figure 4 illustrates the principal ties of capital and the flows of grain which animate the *bharkiwala* enterprise. The rice *aratdar*, the moneylending merchant who purchases the *bharkiwala*'s finished product, provides a working capital loan of *dadon* in return for the pledge of the whole output of the household. The husking mill similarly provides *dadon* to the *bharkiwala*, this time in return for the obligation that all of the paddy processed by the household be milled by it. The third principal tie of trade finance comes from the paddy *aratdar*, a moneylending merchant who provides working capital in the form of paddy. This provision of paddy on credit is incurred under the

FIGURE 4

FINANCIAL ARRANGEMENTS TYING THE SMALL PROCESSOR

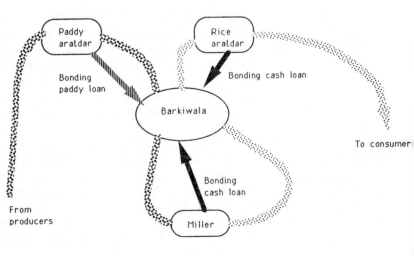

obligation that the *bharkiwala* cannot take paddy from any other source until his debt is repaid.

In some cases, there are further lines of dependence. For example, *bharkiwala*s may take paddy loans from big grower households, and village grocers may also finance a number of *bharkiwala*s supplying rice for their shops. *Bharkiwala*s may also act as agents for moneylending merchants, taking *dhaner upore* loans and on-lending them to poor peasants in a manner analogous to that practised by subordinate traders, described earlier.

Rice and paddy traders and millers in the area each have 20 to 60 *bharkiwala*s tied to them, suggesting a population of at least 100 to 250 *bharkiwala* households in the immediate vicinity of the market commanding the backward area. These small-scale processors operate in the five months after the main *Aman* harvest, with peak throughput in the early, low price weeks immediately after the harvest and declining scale of operation as the price of paddy rises. One rice *aratdar* suggests that 75 per cent of the rice he supplies comes from *bharkiwala*s for the three months after the harvest. Then he has to purchase rice from other parts of the country to supply his network of tied retailers and village grocery shops.

The advance of *dadon* from mills to *bharkiwala*s appears to be an innovation of the last 20 years. As with other backward forms of capital, there is a suggestion that *bharkiwala dadon* has been created by changes in agriculture and trade. In this case the recent extension of tied credit may be associated with the expansion of mechanical milling and the decline of the *bharkiwala*. One miller reports that prior to independence (1971), *bharkiwala*s queued to get their paddy milled. Now, the miller laments, he can only ensure his supply of paddy for milling if he extends *dadon* financing, because the rise of more automated mills has created competition and contributed to the decline of labour-intensive paddy processing.

CONCLUSIONS

The empirical description of trade and agricultural finance in this backward area raises important questions about the future course of social change and the extent to which state policy can contribute to improving the bargaining power of the majority of people in the region. There are a number of developments which may be important in this regard.

The Evolution of Market Competition

Traders from other regions may find commercial margins in the backward area sufficiently attractive to warrant entry into the market. This would require that they provide alternative arrangements for transport, ensure adequate security to undertake trade, and break the hold of merchant moneylenders on that part of marketed grain sold through the latter.

The Outcome of Processes of Accumulation Among Resident Intermediaries

Some resident intermediaries (shopkeepers and subordinate *beparis*) are able to accumulate, both through taking advantage of the margins left in their hands as *dhaner upore* and through appropriating the assets of default-ing *dhaner upore* borrowers. In such cases, resources are sometimes in-vested in production (land and draught animals). This may contribute to the gradual emergence of a group of rich, resident cultivators who will challenge absentee landlords and merchant moneylenders, engaging not only in independent production but also in independent trade.

Expansion of the Supply of Credit

Elite market dominance of the merchant landlord group rests on control of land and control of credit relations. The bank credit which is now available tends to be channelled into financing moneylending merchants. If alterna-tive sources of credit were to be provided, through the extension of bank branches to the area, then that essential element of monopoly could be jeopardised.

Provision of Infrastructure

Creation of a network of adequate roads could also further undermine the transport cartel, and facilitate the entry of competing traders. Dominance in the transport market is made easy by a pattern of roads which funnels almost all motorised transport through the dominant market town. If direct com-munications could be established with alternative centres, the cartel would be more expensive to maintain.

Provision of Drainage, Irrigation and Cheap Inputs

This would constitute another very important, though less direct, challenge to the continuation of the hierarchy.

State policy can play an important role in encouraging one or more of these developments. In fact, road construction is planned for the *char* area. Alternative methods of credit provision, creating innovative institutions for collective supervision of loans, along the lines of the successful Grameen Bank, could also be an important catalyst for change; and challenging the ability of the elite to block smallholder development projects could be another.

Thus there are ways in which the operation of agricultural markets in backward areas could be reformed and economic growth encouraged. Reforms which focus on altering aggregate prices cannot, however, be expected to have a significant influence on the livelihood of the rural poor in regions like the one just described. Of the total foodgrain produced in the *char* area, not more than 30 per cent is directly sold in the market. The remainder is exchanged either as a share payment for land or in repayment of *dhaner upore*. Increasing government support prices for paddy, in such a context, can have very complex and uncertain effects on the majority of producers. Within a structure of forced commerce and interlocked markets, there are grounds to be skeptical about the extent to which absentee landlords and moneylending merchants would pass on any benefits to their clientele.

Obviously, reforms designed to correct state-induced market distortions are equally irrelevant to the livelihood of most agricultural producers in backward areas of Bangladesh. Inefficient markets and misleading price signals exist, but they are created by indigenous commercial agents within a setting of private market regulation, weak state control and only partial commoditisation.

NOTES

1. For a survey of this literature see Crow [*1989*].
2. A Dutch-financed development project in the area, which has increased production through control of irrigation and drainage, has evoked concerted and effective opposition from traders and landowners. This opposition has prevented the successful pilot projected from being replicated. In this case, opposition arises because the project distributes land to landless households and threatens the ability of the elite to control smallholder and tenant production.
3. In an earlier article [*Crow, 1989*], trader–peasant loans (*dhaner upore*) were described as *Dadon I* and trader–trader loans (*dadon*) as *Dadon II*. Both types of capital are sometimes referred to as *dadon*, a word derived from the Persian verb 'to give' suggesting origins in an early contact with colonial commerce. For clarity, we have here adopted the most common local term to distinguish *dhaner upore*.
4. Because of the particular sensitivity of this form of trade, data could only be collected indirectly, through discussions with a number of subordinates of the moneylending trader.
5. Because it compares the *dhaner upore* price with the 'free sale' price received by the same grower in the market, differences of moisture and quality of paddy supply are largely cancelled out.
6. The books of moneylending merchants are particularly confidential. Even the book-keeper has access only to the current ledgers.

REFERENCES

Bhaduri, Amit, 1981, 'Class Relations and the Pattern of Accumulation in an Agrarian Economy', *Cambridge Journal of Economics*, March.

Bhaduri, Amit, 1985, 'Class Relations and Commercialisation in Indian Agriculture: A Study in the Post-Independence Reforms of Uttar Pradesh' in K.N. Raj et al. (eds.), *Essays in the Commercialisation of Indian Agriculture*, New Delhi: Oxford University Press.

Bhaduri, Amit, 1986, 'Forced Commerce and Agrarian Growth', *World Development*, Vol. 14, No. 2.

Bharadwaj, Krishna, 1985, 'A View on Commercialisation in Indian Agriculture and the Development of Capitalism', *Journal of Peasant Studies*, Vol. 12, No. 4.

Crow, Ben, 1989, 'Plain Tales from the Rice Trade: Indications of Vertical Integration in Rice Markets in Bangladesh', *Journal of Peasant Studies*, Vol. 16, No. 2.

Crow, Ben and K.A.S. Murshid, 1989, *The Finance of Forced and Free Markets: Merchants' Capital in the Bangladesh Grain Trade*, DPP/BIDS Working Paper.

Crow, Ben, 1990, 'Moving the Lever: A New Food Aid Imperialism?' in H. Bernstein *et al.* (eds), *The Food Question*, London: Earthscan.

Ellis, F., 1988, *Peasant Economics: Farm Households and Agrarian Development*, Cambridge: Cambridge University Press.

Giasuddin, Md. and Md. A. Hamid, 1986, *Foodgrain Surplus or Deficit Districts and Upazilas of Bangladesh*, Dhaka: Bangladesh Government, Food Planning and Monitoring Unit.

Harriss, B., 1990, 'Another Awkward Class: Merchants and Agrarian Change in India', in H. Bernstein *et al.* (eds.), *The Food Question*, London: Earthscan.

Kabir, N., 1990, 'Poverty, Purdah and Patriarchy: Women's Survival Strategies in Rural Bangladesh' in H. Bernstein *et al.* (eds.), *The Food Question*, London: Earthscan.

Srivastava, R., 1989, 'Interlinked Modes of Exploitation in Indian Agriculture during Transition: A Case Study', *Journal of Peasant Studies*, Vol. 16, No. 4.

World Bank, 1988, *Bangladesh: Adjustment in the Eighties and Short-Term Prospects*, Report 7105–BD (draft), Washington, DC: World Bank.

Real Foodgrains Markets and State Intervention in India

BARBARA HARRISS

Private grain markets in India, like the state regulations applied to them, are among the most complex in the world. This article traces the development of official grain marketing policy, and of real private markets, in three specific regional contexts, and analyses the nexus of bureaucratic and commercial interests influencing actual forms of policy implementation. It forcefully illustrates the inter-connectedness of state and market and explores the impact of state/private marketing structures on patterns of development in different rural contexts.

INTRODUCTION

The discourse of market reform in developing countries in the last decade has been the product of an influential critique of agricultural performance in Sub-Saharan Africa [*World Bank, 1981*]. This critique identified a structural crisis in African agricultural development emanating from inappropriate domestic agricultural and macro-economic policies. Appropriate policies, which became conditions for programmatic financial aid, included (i) adjustment of domestic agricultural prices to align them with international ones (involving progressive phasing out of subsidies, pan-territorial pricing and trade restrictions) and (ii) the liberalisation of marketing systems such that the role of the state in distribution would be reduced to providing infrastructure and information and the role of private trade enlarged.

Experience after adjustment has led to a re-examination of the assumption, taken from theories of comparative advantage and interregional trade, that the invisible hand would provide incentives to, and competitive regulation of, trade; and that it would thereby instantaneously substitute a competitive and efficient allocative mechanism for the previous politically directed, administered, distributive allocations. The process of implementation of deregulation and liberalisation is replete with examples of lagged,

Barbara Harriss, International Development Centre, Queen Elizabeth House, Oxford.

costly, constrained and peculiar responses by 'the market' to trade opportunities.

Features such as the gender division of labour in trade, the asymmetrical distribution and relatively high costs of information, the underdevelopment and overcentralisation of the physical infrastructure of marketing, entry barriers and transaction costs, the prior process of accumulation and savings, the nature of pre-existing (parallel, often inegalitarian and concentrated) structures and relations of commercialisation, as well as the effects of sequencing the component interventions of liberalisation, have variously been invoked to explain the response of markets to deregulation [*Jones and Hay, 1989*; *Kydd and Spooner, 1989*; *Mosley and Smith, 1989*; *Robinson, 1989*; *Scarborough, 1989*]. The slow development and complexity of real markets has also forced a re-evaluation of earlier advocacy of a minimalist regulatory role for the state [*Lele and Christiansen, 1989*].

Facile assumptions about the speed and nature of the response to liberalisation and deregulation by private trade had their origins in particular discourses of development. The neoliberal discourse of market reform, according to Bernstein, manifests a double abstraction; first the abstraction of 'exchange from the totality of relations of production and power' and second a substitution of 'an overarching ideological conception of 'the market' for the analytical, empirical investigation of 'actually existing' markets ... how they are produced by specific historical patterns of commoditisation and how they work' [*1989: 25*]. Bharadwaj, in the course of a critique of neo-classical competitive models of wage determination, notices the same feature, which she explains as a double reductionism; first from relations of production and exchange to 'markets' and second from markets to prices [*Bharadwaj, 1989*]. This article challenges such reductionism, juxtaposing actually existing real markets with real forms of state intervention in India.

In doing this, there is no intention to imply that the reductionism and abstraction of policy discourse is in any sense *unreal*. On the contrary, such reductionism has a real ideological function: in the last analysis it aggrandises the role of the state in economic change and the importance of economistic discourse at the stage of policy-making. As Hewitt de Alcántara says [*1989*], it enables the 'comfortable suggestion of certainty when generalising'. The *lingua franca* of 'policy-making', with its emphasis on *formulation*, permits those who speak it to neglect such areas of concern as the real dynamics of implementation, the nature of actually existing institutions of the market, the nature of the state and the peculiarities of regions [*Schaffer, 1984*; *Mooij, 1989*]. Here it will be suggested that this *lingua franca* may also lead to a misunderstanding of economic processes.

Nowhere would such a misunderstanding be more damaging than with respect to grain – the basis of subsistence and the means of social reproduction – in India as elsewhere. In contrast to much of Africa, grain production in India has kept pace with population growth, and the glaring problems for public policy are now concerned with social and regional distribution [*Clay et al., 1988*]. State regulation of grain distribution is more complex than in Africa, and has hardly to date been touched by adjustment conditionalities.

This paper first examines the historical context and stated intentions of market reform and official intervention, in the interstices of which actual grain markets have evolved on the subcontinent. It then examines the role of grain markets (as moulded by the state) in social reproduction in three agrarian regions with differing exchange environments. After this, the nexus of bureaucratic and commercial interests influencing actual forms of implementation of state policy can be examined, prior to completing the circle by looking at the role in the policy process played by agricultural mercantile politics. Such an exercise should serve to underline the general point – valid for all countries – that grain market reform is an extraordinarily complex task.

GRAIN MARKETING POLICY

The earliest objective of state intervention as it evolved in India after independence was to capture the commanding heights of the economy, from which its lower slopes and less commanding summits could be strategically regulated. The extent of public intervention in private grain markets can be seen as one indication of the latter's strategic position in the economy, for there are on paper a great many tactics for grain market control. These include, first, regulatory measures (public policy on the finance of grain trading; acts which codify transactions in regulated markets; storage and anti-hoarding laws); second, institutions such as co-operatives and storage corporations, competing with private trade; and third, price policy and the necessary institutions of state trading and public distribution which have partially, and in certain regions and time periods completely, replaced private trade.

Trade Finance Policy

Public policy places severe constraints on the lending of money for the finance of private grain trading or inventory holding. Three means have been used: (i) exhortatory and voluntary vigilance against lending by nationalised banks in circumstances where loans might be utilised to underwrite 'hoarding';[1] (ii) mandatory restrictions on the percentage of the value of privately-held grain stock against which loans may be given at specified interest rates (generally regulated commercial rates), as well as ceilings on the length of time for which such loans may be disbursed; and (iii) the residual means of requiring that 60 per cent of total bank deposits obtained from rural and semi-rural areas be lent to 'priority' sectors, not including the grain trade [*Reserve Bank of India, 1980*]. In addition, the state has attempted to channel finance to agricultural producers, through both nationalised commercial banks and co-operative banks, on concessional terms and in such a manner as to compete with private moneylending traders [*Bell, 1990*].

Market Regulation

Market regulation is a low-cost intervention dating from the end of the last century. It was originally aimed at creating conditions of first transaction which were more competitive than would otherwise be the case, in order to raise the producer prices of colonial export crops and effectively to eliminate local autonomy and monopoly in the administration of agricultural market-places. The Regulated Markets Acts were extended (and in certain states they are still being extended) to cover foodgrains and to provide for the participative management of markets by different interest groups, as well as to ensure the regulation of grading and licensing, the provision of systematic price information and the standardisation of weights, measures and fees. These acts establish mechanisms for arbitration in case of disputes and set out requirements for supervising open auction and payment; and they define the need for physical infrastructure, such as stores and assembly yards, for particular crops over a given spatial territory [*Harriss, 1984: 71–115*].

Co-operative Marketing

Like market regulation, marketing co-operatives have a history going back to the early part of the century. They were envisioned (in both the rural credit surveys of the Reserve Bank of India and the Foodgrain Enquiry Committee Reports of the 1950s) as the central elements in a socialised trading sector, where transactions could take place in regulated open markets through networks of small marketing co-operatives. The latter were in fact to eradicate the middleman [*Nehru, 1970: 384–6*], an institutional possibility which is specifically allowed for in the later Regulated Markets Acts.

In time, most co-operatives lost their financial independence and decentralised participative management, and became anchored at the base of hierarchical structures controlled by state government departments and by the National Co-operative Development Board. (This latter institution, set up in 1956, has been responsible *inter alia* for financing co-operative marketing.) Of late, marketing has come to form only one part of schemes to promote co-operative management and development through provision by the National Co-operative Development Board of all components of production, from extension and advisory services through inputs and raw materials to product sales and processing [*Clay et al., 1988*].

Public Sector Storage

Public policy in the field of grain storage has evolved in response to four main arguments. First, traditional storage technology was thought to be associated with high losses, which the state could lower with modern technology. Second, stores located in rural areas were thought necessary to break the constraint of producers' low holding capacity [*Rudra, 1983*]. Third, such producers could then be assisted to reduce distress sales through provision by the state of low-interest credit against stored commodities, upon presentation by the borrower of a receipt for stored crops; and this service would strengthen the bargaining power of producers against merchants [*Shadakshataradhya, 1977*]. Fourth, the amplitude of seasonal price fluctuations could be reduced and producers would receive higher wholesale prices.

On recommendation of the All India Rural Credit Survey of 1954, the Agricultural Produce (Development and Warehouse) Act of 1956 empowered the central government to draw on Reserve Bank funds for warehouse construction; and in the 1960s and 1970s, warehousing corporations came into existence, first at a national and then at state levels [*National Co-operative Development Corporation, 1976*]. Now that official institutions control nearly 40 million tonnes of storage, contemporary policy has turned to relocation and decentralisation.

Price Policy

Policy on agricultural prices has involved non-monopolistic, but pan-territorial pricing, administered at a national level, with a small amount of discretionary latitude in price setting by states. The policy has had two declared purposes. One is to hold down the prices of essential commodities, among which grain is of paramount importance. The other, more recent, is to use changes in the structure of administered prices to encourage a balance within the foodgrain sector between production of cereals (in surplus) and production of pulses and oilseeds (in deficit).

The Agricultural Costs and Prices Commission fixes procurement or minimum support prices for cereals, groundnuts, sugar, gram, pulses and key agro-industrial crops. Pan-territorial prices are calculated on the basis of (i) increasingly systematised cost of production surveys, (ii) aggregate input/output ratios, (iii) product price ratios, (iv) desired and planned changes in land use and (v) world market prices, as well as political consultation with interest groups (including research institutions, state governments and relevant ministries) [*Clay et al., 1988*; *Sidhu, 1986*].

State Trading

Price policy is implemented both through co-operatives (which are not constrained to sell only at the official support price but can also trade at open market prices) and, far more importantly, through government trading institutions, including the central government's Food Corporation of India (FCI) and the trading corporations of many constituent states.

The history of this arrangement dates back to the Second World War, when supply shortages led the Food Department to set up a series of Foodgrain Policy Committees to advise on means of performing its mandate to distribute food nationally. The committees recommended soon after independence that the stabilisation of grain prices, the management of a buffer stock and 'the elimination of the middleman in the foodgrains trade' required an independent corporation. In 1957, the Foodgrain Enquiry Committee reaffirmed the potential of state trading as an act of socialisation in its own right and as a means of controlling the behaviour of the wholesale trade through imports and buffer stocks. But the idea of an autonomous organisation was dismissed as stimulating the development of vested interests and delaying the participative socialisation of exchange by co-operatives.

Even now aspects of trade policy such as restrictions on the movement of grain are under the aegis of state government food departments, rather than that of the central authorities. Notwithstanding, the FCI was born in 1965 with a brief which is sufficiently comprehensive for it to replace private trade if ordered, and to compete with it if not. These powers were enhanced by granting the FCI the right to act as a credit agency both for production loans and for borrowing by farmers against post-harvest stocks [*Harriss, 1984: 117–74*; *Sidhu, 1986*].

Grain procured by the Food Corporation of India or by state-level grain trading parastatals is disbursed in two ways. The first is in the form of emergency relief, which over time has been systematised, extended to cover certain kinds of seasonal or permanent distribution, and diversified as nutrition or employment schemes. The second involves contributions to a more permanently organised low (or 'fair') price distribution system providing subsidised grain to certain locations and defined categories of consumer 'according to need'. The former have tended to be urban and/or border areas, with wider spatial coverage in deficit states. Consumers have been targetted by income (low) and by occupation (for example, the families of policemen). This public distribution system is justified not only as a welfare measure, involving a subsidy to a basic wage good, but also as exerting deflationary pressure on open market retail prices affecting a broader constituency.

Certain observations about this system of interventions are in order. First, the intentions of these reforms have over the years been consistently transformational and anti-mercantilist, in the sense of creating wide-ranging powers to curb private agricultural trade. None of the interventions proposed was intended to benefit private commerce.

Second, intended beneficiaries have for the most part been described as undifferentiated 'agricultural producers'. Regulated markets are supposed to protect the prices received by 'small farmers' and to facilitate their participation in market management. State trading is not only to raise producer prices to support levels but also to provide production credit to those with a marketed surplus. It was originally hoped that marketing co-operatives would raise and stabilise producer prices, and co-operatives were claimed to have the additional advantages of being decentralised, participative and consistent with a range of market and non-market modes of operation. In addition, state warehousing at the outset had the unambiguous purpose of enabling farmers to gain access to state credit upon production of a warehouse receipt.

Third, while never justifying interventions as arising from extremes of market failure, those responsible for enabling legislation have never seemed to be much convinced that markets work efficiently either. They have been concerned with imperfect markets and the institutional minutiae of their regulation from the time of the first appearance of reports dealing with the marketing of each major agricultural commodity. (There was abundant case study evidence dating from the 1930s.)

Fourth, these interventions were a phased but not a co-ordinated assault upon the private market. In Tamil Nadu, for example, regulated markets legislation was enacted in 1933. Public grain procurement and public distribution started during and has continued intermittently since the Second World War, though the state trading corporations came into being much later (FCI in 1965 and the Tamil Nadu State Civil Supplies Corporation in 1972). Marketing co-operatives were set up in the 1950s, state storage schemes from 1965. State curbs on the finance of private grain trading date from the nationalisation of commercial banks in 1969. Schemes of payment in kind from state grain stocks to rural labour started in 1978. This gradual encroachment took place in a piecemeal fashion and was in no way the product of deliberate planning. Grain markets have developed historically alongside this edifice of state intervention and legislation.

ACTUALLY EVOLVING GRAIN MARKETS

Markets perform ambivalent roles in social reproduction. By signalling prices, they are at one and the same time institutions of resource allocation in marketing and the means by which resources may be allocated in production. *Allocatively efficient* markets lead to increases in aggregate agricultural commodity production, as well as to specialisation and inter-regional integration according to principles of comparative advantage. But by syphoning off resources (classically through buying and selling, but as shall be shown, also through other modalities of surplus extraction) markets may route potentially reinvestible resources away from productive deployment in agriculture. *Class efficient* markets are those which structure the process of secondary appropriation and redistribution of surplus in such a way as to perpetuate a dominant commercial class, which may deprive direct producers of some or all of the means of expanded reproduction [*Bhaduri, 1986*].

Money entirely locked up in marketing, in buying and selling, is not productive capital, even though it is necessary for social reproduction. But agricultural merchants' capital is hardly ever found in its pure form. It is commonly mingled with productive capital (invested in activities such as processing, transport and quality-maintaining storage), constituting an essential element of circulation and accumulation. It is mixed, in commercial portfolios, with industrial and agricultural capital. Furthermore, by means of interlocked contracts on credit and product markets, it is often associated with usurers' or finance capital. In a practical sense, then, 'commercial capital' is usually productive and agricultural commercial capital is not independent of production relations. It can change agrarian classes and be changed by them. Analysis of the ambivalent social roles of agricultural commercial capital, within the evolving network of regulatory legislation in three regions of India, may illustrate this point more clearly.[2]

North Arcot District

Located on the flat Coromandel Plain towards the southeastern seaboard of India, this region has witnessed a striking technical transformation of rice production since the early 1970s, involving a 50 per cent rise in output and a doubling of yields within a decade. This expansion has been based to a great extent on the exploitation of groundwater through the electrification of open wells. The productivity of land and labour have both increased without a transformation of production relations.

The agrarian class structure has for a long while been characterised by a small landed elite, a numerically important smallholding peasantry, a large landless labour force and a relatively large 'residual' group engaged in non-agricultural activity. The region has experienced countervailing trends in household mobility, especially marked among the poor peasantry, where households losing land are matched by landless households gaining land. A modest amount of migration out of the region and diversification out of agriculture, into non-agricultural wage work and petty production, has occurred among the poor peasantry, while branches of rich peasant and capitalist households have diversified their non-agricultural investment options (under speculative rather than distress conditions), putting money into the urban and rural non-farm economy and employing rural commuters and migrants in these urban enterprises. The agrarian system thus uses a constant number of people in agriculture to support an increasing population in the non-agricultural economy, especially in the sphere of circulation.

The region has seen a commercial explosion, creating crowded marketing systems. Although social barriers such as gender and caste debar about 75 per cent of the local population from wholesale trading, the economic barriers to entry into retail/petty trade are low. Nevertheless, accumulation in the latter sector is checked by a variety of factors. First, there are dependent ties of credit between small and large trading firms. Second, small firms have relatively higher per unit trading and transaction cost components than larger ones. Third, the consumption requirements of traders' households constrain accumulation and even drag a minority of such firms below the poverty line. The commercial sector is thus polarised, and effective control over commodity exchange is highly concentrated.

In fact, although the commercial sector in North Arcot still elides with the landed upper class, merchant capital is progressively becoming separated from its agriculturally productive origins. As yet, however, non agro-industrial entrepreneurship is not evident in the commercial sector (except for urban real estate, where merchants are very active); and capitalist relations in agro-industry are qualified by a number of factors. There is, for example, a pervasive reliance on family labour in small firms, which tend more toward a simple-commodity than a capitalist type; and within the sub-set of firms which do employ wage workers, debt is tactically deployed in order to constrain the development of a free labour market. Women are required to work particularly long hours for extremely low pay, and their employment opportunities are restricted to the field of casual labour. Throughout the sphere of circulation, merchant and moneylending capital is fused.

The compulsion of smallholding peasants to borrow, not only for consumption but also for production, has been intensified by the cash component of the new technology [*J. Harriss, 1990*]. These debt relationships then constrain the timing and location, as well as the intermediary, through which debtors sell. Strictly speaking, such ties do not pertain to quantities over and above those needed for repayment. Nevertheless moneylending merchants often receive more of a crop than is formally required to cancel a debt, through relying on the inertia of the debtor, who anticipates future contractual favours as a reward for faithfulness.

It has been argued that such relations of indebtedness and tied exchange lead to depeasantisation and dispossession of land, and to the enlargement of the rural proletariat. But this process is hardly visible in North Arcot because, for a number of reasons, it is not rational for merchants to foreclose on land. In the first place, assumption of legal possession is costly; and there are management constraints and supervision costs involved in farming on foreclosed property. Furthermore, ties of caste, which exist in an estimated half of all transactions, make it difficult to engage in coercive behaviour. And most important, agricultural production is simply less profitable than marketing and moneylending.

Both small and large traders lend money, insisting on repayment in kind in order to guarantee supplies at the lowest, post harvest prices.[3] With these supplies, traders then speculate. Just as debt relations restrict the development of markets in labour and land under such circumstances, so the lower rates of return inherent in debt relations reduce the profitability of expanding the land base of a portfolio, even in technically efficient enterprises. Thus the capitalist transformation of agricultural production is checked; and merchant capital reproduces forms of peasant production in North Arcot District.[4] At one level this is an efficient process and functional for capital, taking advantage of the propensity of the peasants to exploit their own labour. Yet in locking up potentially investible surplus for speculative activity on markets, such mercantile deployment of capital constrains the development of productive capitalism.

Coimbatore District

This is a dry frontier plains region, abutting the Nilgiri hills of Tamil Nadu. Although historically in deficit for foodgrains (grown on rainfed land which has resisted technological transformation), the region is endowed with a diversified and long-commoditised agricultural economy, and boasts a well-developed class of farmers managing relatively highly capitalised enterprises. It also has a long-standing and large rural proletariat, engaged in rural industry as well as agriculture – a feature which the development of the home market will not support in more than a few locations on the subcontinent. Agricultural producers are experiencing rising debt burdens, lowering water tables and a squeeze in the relationship between costs and prices.

Here the commercial class is numerically small and engaged not only in local trade but also in long distance trade on the national market. In the latter case, barriers to entry are formidable. Thus in Coimbatore there is even greater polarisation of trading assets, of gross output and of mercantile control over agricultural land and commodity storage than in North Arcot. Within a universe of business strategies composed of complex combinations of productive and unproductive activity, each trading firm is likely to fashion a unique set.

For the merchants of Coimbatore, agriculture is less important as a source of investment in trade, and secondary appropriation through agricultural commerce is more important, than for counterparts in North Arcot. Except in the case of the main agro-industrial raw material of the region (cotton), moneylending is not linked to trading. Even when it is, repayment can be in cash at predetermined and explicit rates of interest, and debt does not bind the commodity transactions of borrower and merchant. Agricultural mercantile firms are commonly part of complex commercial and industrial portfolios, which manifest both horizontal and vertical linkages.

The role of merchant capital in reproducing agrarian society in Coimbatore appears to be quite limited. The latter is not affected by indirect control over production of the means of subsistence (through indebtedness) as it is in North Arcot, and the monetary needs of rural people can be met through a variety of non-mercantile activities, such as wage labour, usually involving payment in cash and self-employment. Such mercantile power as does exist in the agrarian society of Coimbatore operates through tightly concentrated control over stored (imported) grain for preharvest distress consumption by the rural landless labour force, to whom mercantile credit is extended. Surplus is also syphoned away from agricultural producers and consumers by means of economic crime. Fraud on weights and measures, arbitrary deductions, closed transactions, delayed payments and collusive price fixing are practised against producers; and fraud on weights and measures, as well as adulteration, against consumers. Illegally low wages and illegal recourse to casual labour affect the work force. Finally, bureaucratic corruption supports fraudulent activities among merchants, creating a nexus of powerful interests characteristic of capitalism in this area.

Birbhum District

It is useful to turn now to a backward rice producing district in West Bengal. Here the riskiness of grain production is similar to that prevailing in dry tracts of Coimbatore. New production technology is not widely available because of the singular vulnerability of the region to increasingly frequent droughts and floods; nor could new technologies be rapidly adopted in the situation of widespread and grinding poverty characteristic of agricultural society in this area. The average income from rice cultivation in Birbhum District is on a par with that to be obtained from labouring in North Arcot.

The region was formerly a classic site of semi-feudal production relations, in which a small landlord class controlled markets for land, labour, grain and money. Rental shares were generally fixed at a level high enough to render sharecroppers dependent upon landlords for both production and consumption credit, which was repaid in kind. Surplus appropriated through rent and debt repayments left a net stock insufficient to ensure the independent survival of most direct producers. This surplus was then available for speculative trading.

Land reforms have recently turned sharecroppers into a simple-commodity producing peasantry, but they have not changed the landed power of the rich peasantry and small landlord class whose properties could be shown to be under the land reform ceilings. Furthermore, property ownership other than land has not been touched by the reforms and survives from the pre-reform era more or less intact. Therefore the appropriation of paddy in this agrarian society continues to support an enormous edifice of credit and trade. At the apex of the marketing system is a handful of magnates whose firms are characterised by highly exploitive internal relations (extremely low wages and bonded contracts are common in these establishments). At the base of the marketing system is a growing crowd of unlicensed and therefore illegal petty traders, often women and often relying on family labour. In Africa, this might be called parallel trade. In West Bengal, such illegal trade runs parallel not only to institutions of state trading but also to institutions of legal private trade.

Agricultural surpluses are important sources of investment capital in the middle and lower, semi-legal echelons of the commercial sector, but these surpluses are appropriated through rent rather than through profits on direct production, using wage labour. A central element in the process of appropriation at higher levels is to be found in the oligopolistic position of rice mills, which make money through renting property, water and land, and through usury, as well as in the course of obtaining agro-industrial profits. A part of their strategy of accumulation is also based on fraudulent manipulation of volumetric measures and weights, misinformation about prices, arbitrary deductions, delayed and uncompensated payments – all aspects of primitive accumulation. On the whole, however, the importance of grain in the commercial, financial and industrial portfolios of the largest firms of Birbhum District is dwindling.

The mass of the peasantry in the region is no longer as likely to be exploited through payment of rent as it was in pre-land reform times, but it continues to produce a surplus which is extracted by moneylending merchants operating in a hierarchy of tied credit and commodity relations. At the base, these relations are manifested in consumption loans to be repaid in kind. The deliveries of grain which are pledged against these loans in turn fuel a process of profiteering at all levels of the trading structure. In the case of West Bengal, this process is shaped by a singular fact: since the state needs the grain oligopoly to facilitate the supply of grain on quota for the public distribution system of Calcutta, it has conferred a legislative monopoly over the wholesale trade upon a small group of magnates and has subsidised the modernisation of their milling technology. Such protection leads to wider distributive margins in marketing than can be found in either North Arcot or Coimbatore, thus attracting the swarm of smaller illegal intermediaries. The rates of return which the latter can expect are, however, sharply constrained by the requirement that they pay bribes to vigilance forces. Furthermore, in the course of earning their own living, small illegal traders divert supplies from the oligopoly and threaten the state-controlled food supply system.

Despite tenurial gains, then, the livelihood of the mass of peasant producers in this relatively backward region is still dependent upon the coalesced power of landlords, merchants and usurers. Cultivators operating in the context of such strong mechanisms of surplus appropriation are deprived of resources for accumulation and investment in agriculture. They have not been released from debt bondage through land reform, since tenurial reform cannot by itself alter the structure of dependence mediated through the markets.

Lessons from the Case Studies

Although each case discussed above has unique features, with important implications for policy and for politics, certain general comments are now in order. First, it should be clear that the markets just described are far from resembling those of advanced capitalism, let alone the textbook archetypes of competitive markets. To begin with, there are limits to commodity relations in the operation of mercantile firms themselves. These limits are most dramatically manifest in the internal organisation of the latter, where payments in kind, particularistic systems of cash or kind 'perks', the debt bonding of employees and the use of unremunerated household labour defy the organisation of workers in 'markets'.

With regard to the commoditised exchange of grain, the ubiquity of accumulation through coercive and/or illegal practices is noteworthy (even if the issue of the anti-social nature of some laws is both separate and contentious). Furthermore, the preceding case studies illustrate the basic point that *grain markets are not atomistic*. They are highly concentrated and polarised, as are the markets for the transport of grain. Entry into some areas of the marketing system may be constrained by sizeable economic barriers, and gender and caste constrain entry almost everywhere.

In addition, *grain markets are not impersonal*, being riven instead with particularistic economic and social ties emanating commonly from debt relations and from caste connections. *Prices are not normally set through the working of a smoothly equilibrating mechanism*. In fact, strong conventions underlie the setting of minimum net profits; collusive oligopolies commonly coexist with price-taking firms; short-term price fluctuations over time and space can be considerable and lead to high rates of return for merchants with information, contacts and access to modern transport and processing technology. Lastly, *the 'market' is not independent of relations of production* and plays a role in the formation of classes. The meshing of commercial capital with productive industrial and agricultural capital means that mercantile accumulation cannot be distinguished from accumulation generally.

In northern Tamil Nadu (North Arcot), for example, commercial capital, pervasively interlinked with production credit, has induced a certain level of technological modernisation in agriculture, through facilitating the use of fertilisers and pesticides on smallholdings; but at the same time it has constrained the social transformation of agriculture in the region by reproducing (both actively and by default) a variety of forms of peasant production. In southern Tamil Nadu (Coimbatore), on the other hand, grain merchants are not involved in extending production credit, and agricultural production relations have long taken capitalist forms. Commercial accumulation has led directly to investment in, and expansion of, the local non-farm rural economy. And in Birbhum District of West Bengal, a very backward form of debt bondage has survived land reform, as a landlord-moneylender-trader class has altered the weighting of the various modes through which it extracts resources from producers.

IMPLEMENTED POLICY

In practice, it is also impossible to separate these real markets from the evolving apparatus of state intervention, not only because the latter regulates markets but also because merchants become a part of state institutions and are often successful in manipulating official interventions so that these coincide with their own interests. Here, in order to expand these points, our discussion is general rather than confined to particular regions.[5]

The Finance of Trade

It is unlikely that the Indian state can avoid financing private trade in foodgrains, despite declared intentions and legislation to the contrary.

Taking advantage of the fungibility of credit, trading interests obtain loans ostensibly earmarked for small-scale industry or, most commonly, for agricultural production, and then invest this money in commerce. Merchants also obtain credit on grain stocks if the latter are stored in public sector warehouses; and they have gained access to international funds, from the IDA through the Agro Refinance Development Corporation of India, for private warehouse construction as well.

Market Regulation

Regulation has proceeded unevenly by region and by crop. For example, all crops in the poverty belt in the north-east of India are strikingly poorly regulated; and wherever they are found, foodgrains tend to be among the last crops to be covered by the regulatory acts. Furthermore, small-scale trade is excluded from the purview of the Acts, as is moneylending.

Only a very small percentage of all market transactions in grain take place in a manner congruent with market regulations, which often are ignored by government trading institutions and monopoly business houses alike. Vigilance on the part of public officials is incommensurate with the physical and economic size of agricultural markets; and in addition, mechanisms for resolving disputes have been weak and biased toward the interests of merchants. Over time, grain markets have therefore been run on a progressively more centralised and less participative basis.

Intervention by the state tends to succeed best where private trade is anyway reasonably competitive, and where production credit is not provided by merchants. These are, however, unusual marketing conditions. In general, the work of Regulated Market Committees seems to centre around collection of fees from traders on an *ad valorem* basis, in return for more or less well-provided Regulated Market Services. The intervention can be highly profitable, but it does not promote competitive pricing in grain markets.

Co-operative Marketing

Grain has not been the forte of marketing co-operatives, which have tended to handle fruit and vegetables, cotton, tobacco, sugar, milk and plantation crops, either for small and medium-sized commercial farmers or under conditions of considerable indirect subsidy to organised peasants. In the case of grain marketing co-operatives, grain merchants frequently play a prominent role on the boards of directors of these local institutions and affect their trading decisions. Perhaps for such reasons, grain marketing co-operatives have often lost their financial independence and decentralised management and are controlled by state government departments and by the National Co-operative Development Corporation (the NCDC).

The NCDC runs at a very slim net surplus, though it required net subsidies in the 1960s and 1970s. It has funded innovations in agro-processing (rice, oil and dhal mills) which are intended to provide benefits to co-operatives; but the large scale and concomitantly high break-even points associated with the prevailing technology have implied frequent losses. The fact that such mills are restricted to operating within a framework of administered prices, rather than higher open market ones, further weakens their financial position. In these circumstances it is not unusual to find that marketing co-operatives do not make use of inefficient co-operative processing facilities, but contract instead to deal with privately owned plants.

Storage

By 1988, the capacity of central and state warehousing corporations had expanded to the level of some fifteen million tonnes. In addition, co-operatives had a storage capacity of eight million tonnes, the FCI twelve million tonnes and state trading corporations eight million tonnes. Even more warehouse construction was planned, to replace outdated storage technology, to decentralise and to secure storage at points of intersection between road transport and narrow- and broad-gauge lines of rail. Farmers themselves have nevertheless not had much recourse to stored grain as collateral for credit: records in South India show that the use of state-owned storage is dominated by state institutions and by large private merchants. In addition, private traders own warehouses with an estimated capacity of about 20 million tonnes of grain, at least a quarter of which has been financed by the World Bank [*Clay et al., 1988*].

Price Policy

Administered prices for grains have varied in a way which imitates, in broad brush, the evolution of prices on the open market. In fact, the relative power of lobbies representing the various regulated cereals (wheat, rice and millets) tends to be reflected in the relative prices of these crops in both open and administered markets. Thus wheat has historically been granted a higher procurement price than other regulated cereals, and this benefits the powerful class of capitalist farmers which dominates supply in regions where grain is procured by official agencies directly from producers.

Price policy also varies regionally in its impact. The fact that regulation hinges upon the activities of state trading institutions and their agents, which have limited procurement capacities in many areas, has meant that, often, the proportion of marketed surplus officially procured is too small to affect the aggregate agricultural/non-agricultural terms of trade, to counter adverse input/output price relationships or to influence trends toward increasing regional variability in the terms of trade, which have contributed to widening inter-regional inequality in agricultural productivity.

Official agencies engage in mandatory procurement of a set proportion of traded grain, through what is termed a 'levy'. This procurement is quite commonly effected from traders, rather than from producers, and at prices below those of the open market. Traders then make compensating increases in the prices of unlevied grain. When further intraseasonal increases in the proportion levied at relatively low administered prices are announced, traders can only calculate their loss on levied rice against a residual market price already distorted by previous compensatory increases. Open market prices are thus progressively distorted upward. Wholesale markets are also prey to further inflationary forces because of the impact on prices of a reduction in supplies in the regions where procurement is carried out.

Although the purpose of mandatory procurement is to benefit needy consumers, it should be obvious that processes of the kind just described can have very harmful effects on poor net buyers of grain who do not have access to the public distribution system. The latter developed historically as a minimally targeted urban rationing scheme for deficit areas. Only recently has it been expanded to include programmes in districts where a surplus of grain is produced. In areas where it is still not in place, the rural landless labour force and marginal smallholders, as well as the non-rural low-income population, are penalised.

State Trading

About 30 per cent of marketed grain is controlled in some way by the state in India. The FCI has expanded exponentially since its start, as have the state trading corporations, although on a relatively much smaller scale. The FCI now exports grain, albeit intermittently, instead of importing as earlier; and in the internal market, it has diversified into pulses, sugar and fertiliser.

Its power is nevertheless circumscribed by other state institutions and by private merchants. The price policy which it implements is, for example, entirely out of its control, since that policy is set independently by the Agricultural Costs and Prices Commission. This has led to gluts in wheat and to the need to expand storage, in a development not unrelated to the power of the wheat lobby, mentioned earlier. At the same time, in order to reduce fixed and variable procurement costs and increase operational flexibility, the FCI has had to draw private traders into the official marketing circuit as processors and agents. These private traders in turn benefit in various ways: they can re-route working capital, originally provided by the state, toward

their own businesses, utilise subsidised credit to finance technical innovations, and illegally trade part of contracted output. They also enjoy reduced
risks when working at least partially within the official marketing structure.

Restrictions on the movement of traded goods have been intermittently
enforced by public authorities in India. When misimplemented, this policy
can benefit a nexus of private merchants and lower-level bureaucrats, as
traders reap excess profits from price differentials between surplus districts
(where prices are artificially low) and deficit districts (where prices are
artificially high because of supply constraints). Bureaucrats and vigilance
forces benefit through bribery and corruption.

Despite its commitment to an ideology of technical and economic transformation through planning and regulation, the state acts ambivalently
towards the commercial sector in the three regions of our case studies. In
North Arcot, it uses price structures to subsidise peasant production and has
promoted the transformation of production techniques, but it is nevertheless implicated in maintaining relations of indirect commercial control which
constrain the transformation of production relations. In West Bengal, the
state has greatly strengthened peasant forms of production through land
reform. At the same time, it relies on and subsidises the mercantile oligopoly
which perpetuates exploitive exchange relations in the region. Everywhere,
including Coimbatore, some government agents profit privately both from
indirect control by traders over the production process and from the
subversion of state intervention in the way described earlier.

MERCANTILE POLITICS

Merchants are not easy to identify as a class because of the complexity of
their activity and the great heterogeneity of the units comprising 'the
market'. Nevertheless, as already suggested in our discussion of
implemented interventions, traders do act politically to defend their mercantile interests, obscure though their *modus operandi* may be. In India,
they do not operate in a conspicuous way through the prevailing party
political machine: either they are not politically active, or their activity spans
all parties. An important manifestation of mercantile political activity is in
fact the funding of a very wide range of parties.

The power of agricultural merchants in India is expressed through local
social and political institutions, such as temple administrations (through
which they can control urban land); panchayats and co-operatives (which
enable them to interact with and try to control the bureaucracy); philan-
thropic societies such as the Lions and Rotary (which not only provide a
status arena but also publicity and contacts with other interest groups).
Their most powerful means of political action is, however, through com-

modity associations or lobbies. These are ubiquitously and assiduously organised. They come into being in response to threats to profits from organised labour and from the state; and they respond as well to a need for private regulation and physical protection of long distance trade. Such associations often have influence over the bureaucracy, police and judiciary. They are instruments of collective action with a contradictory effect: they are necessary for the development of markets; but, by restricting entry, they simultaneously constrain that development.[6]

The conflict between the regulating state and regulated commerce is in consequence far more apparent than real. There is a strong coincidence of interest between merchants and the state in the special misimplementations of policies which create institutional rent, on the one hand, and excess profit on the other. There is also much direct enlistment of trading groups into the state apparatus. Furthermore, the state cannot avoid granting invisible subsidies to the mercantile sector, particularly through the redirection of credit, despite policy statements to the contrary. Finally, there would seem to be newly abundant and increasingly close ties of kinship between merchants and bureaucrats; and this is an element which deserves close attention when discussing a supposed dichotomy between state and market in India.

Resistance to mercantile power, were it desired, could hardly be expected from compromised institutions of the state. Instead it seems to await challenges from industrial or agricultural capital, or labour.

POSTSCRIPT

It is far easier to identify the lessons from these Indian examples than to assess their ramifications for other parts of the world. The deregulation and liberalisation of markets will never occur under *tabula rasa* conditions. Existing marketing arrangements will be varied and specific. They will have histories. Their structure and functioning will rarely comply with the basic assumptions of neo-classical economic theories, or even with the expectations of national policy-makers. Steps may nominally be taken to ensure competitive markets, regulated by the state, or to supplant uncompetitive markets with state programmes, or to divest the state of all responsibility for the market. In none of these instances is it likely that implemented policy emanating from any declared position will operate in the way foreseen in original statements of intention.

It is clear that complex, real arrangements for commodity marketing and the processes of accumulation which shape them need to be understood before policies are uttered and implemented. This much was grasped by colonial British powers in India in the early part of this century, when they commissioned a series of regional studies of agricultural markets in order to provide a factual basis for intervention. The colonial administration later went on, however, to disregard local reality and to impose regulatory laws designed for British rather than for Indian society (and in the end never implemented in Britain). The lesson of their failure may be instructive for the current government, as it begins to carry out the reforms associated with a new structural adjustment loan, and its attendant conditionalities.

NOTES

1. 'Hoarding' denotes storage in excess of legal limits on the quantity of grain which can be held by a private merchant, and/or lack of observance of limits which have been fixed on the length of time during which grain can be withheld from the market.
2. Material is drawn from the following studies: B. Harriss [*1981; 1990*], for North Arcot; [*1985; 1991a*] for Coimbatore; and [*1982*] for West Bengal.
3. See the article by Ben Crow and K.A.S. Murshid, in this collection, for a detailed analysis of tied lending in the context of Bangladesh.
4. Peasant production has been defined in various ways. Ellis' [*1988*] discussion is helpful here. The peasantry relies in large part (although not necessarily exclusively) on family labour to produce goods for own consumption, as well as for sale. The peasant household, as both consumption and production unit, faces incomplete and imperfect markets. The peasantry occupies a subordinate position in relation to other classes and/or to the state.
5. For such a discussion, see B. Harriss [*1984*].
6. See B. Harriss [*1991b*] for a full description of institutions which regulate collective action among merchants in another district (Burdwan) of West Bengal.

REFERENCES

Bell, C., 1990, 'Interaction between Institutional and Informal Credit in Rural India', *World Bank Economic Review*, 4 (Sept.), pp. 297–327.
Bernstein, H., 1989, *Agricultural Modernisation in the Era of Structural Adjustment*, Development Policy and Practice Discussion Paper, Milton Keynes: Open University.
Bhadhuri, A., 1986, 'Forced Commerce and Agrarian Change', *World Development*, Vol. 14, No. 2.
Bharadwaj, K., 1989, *On the Formation of the Labour Market in Rural Asia*, Geneva: International Labour Office.
Clay, E.J., Benson, C., Harriss B. and S. Gillespie, 1988, *Food Strategy in India* (2 vols.), London: Relief and Development Institute.
Ellis, F., 1988, *Peasant Economics*, Cambridge: Cambridge University Press.
Harriss, B., 1981, *Transitional Trade and Rural Development*, New Delhi: Vikas.
Harriss, B., 1984, *State and Market*, New Delhi: Concept.
Harriss, B., 1985, 'Agricultural Markets and Intersectoral Resource Transfers: Cases from the Semi Arid Tropics of Southeast India', in ICRISAT: *Agricultural Markets in the Semi Arid Tropics*, Hyderabad: ICRISAT.
Harriss, B., 1990, 'The Arni Studies: Changes in the Private Sector of a Market Town', in P. Hazell and C.S. Ramasamy (eds.), *Green Revolution Reconsidered: A Study of the High Yielding Varieties in South India*, Baltimore, MD: Johns Hopkins University Press.
Harriss, B., 1991a, *Masters of the Countryside: A Regional Political Economy of Agricultural*

Markets in an Advanced District of South India, Report to ODA, London (Queen Elizabeth House, Oxford).

Harriss, B., 1991b, *State, Market and Society: Problems of Agricultural Marketing under Conditions of Smallholder Agriculture in West Bengal*, Report to WIDER, Helsinki (Queen Elizabeth House, Oxford).

Harriss, J., 1990, 'What Happened to the Green Revolution in North Arcot? Economic Trends, Household Mobility and the Politics of an "Awkward Class" ', in P. Hazell and C.S. Ramasamy (eds.), *Green Revolution Reconsidered: A Study of the High Yielding Varieties in South India*, Baltimore, MD: Johns Hopkins University Press.

Hewitt de Alcántara, C., 1989, 'Food Pricing and Market Reforms: Social and Political Issues', Paper prepared for the Seminar on Food Pricing and Marketing Reforms convened by UNRISD, Geneva, 20–22 Nov. 1989.

Jones, S. and R. Hay, 1989, *Food Market Reform in Tanzania, Malawi and Zambia*, Oxford: Food Studies Group.

Kydd, J. and N. Spooner, 1989, 'Agricultural Market Liberalisation and Structural Adjustment in Sub Saharan Africa', Paper prepared for the Seminar on Food Marketing Policy Adjustment, FAO, Dar Es Salaam, 1989.

Lele, U. and R.E. Christiansen, 1989, *Markets, Marketing Boards and Co-operatives in Africa: Issues in Adjustment Policy*, Madia Discussion Paper 11, Washington, DC: World Bank.

Mooij, J., 1989, *Food Policy and State Form: Comparative Research in Two South Indian States*, Wageningen: Agricultural Research Group, Agricultural University.

Mosley, P. and L. Smith, 1989, 'Structural Adjustment and Agricultural Performance in Sub Saharan Africa, 1980–1987', *Journal of International Development*, Vol.1, No.3.

National Co-operative Development Corporation, 1976, *Annual Report*, New Delhi.

Nehru, J., 1970, 'Co-operation', in D. Deshmukh (ed.), *Action for Rural Change*, Delhi: Munshiram Manoharlal.

Reserve Bank of India, 1980, *Report on the Trend and Progress of Banking in India*, Supplement to *Reserve Bank of India Bulletin*, Bombay.

Robinson, P., 1989, 'Structural Adjustment in the Rice Sector in Madagascar', Paper prepared for the 10th Seminar on Rural Economy, CIRAD, Montpelier, 1989.

Rudra, A., 1983, 'On the Non-Maximising Behaviour of Indian Farmers', *Economic and Political Weekly*, Vol.48, No.26.

Scarborough, V., 1989, *Food Marketing Post-Liberalisation in Malawi and Tanzania*, London: Wye College of Agriculture.

Schaffer, B.B., 1984, 'Towards Responsibility: Public Policy in Concept and Practice', in E. Clay and B.B. Schaffer (eds.), *Room for Manoeuvre*, London: Heinemann.

Shadakshataradhya, G.C., 1977, 'The Role of the Central Warehousing Corporation with Special Reference to Karnataka', M.Sc. thesis, Mysore: IDS.

Sidhu, D.S., 1986, 'Policies Pertaining to Agricultural Marketing and Input Supply', in Indian Society of Agricultural Economics (ed.), *Agricultural Development: The Next Stage*, Bombay: Himalaya Publishing House.

World Bank, 1981, *Accelerated Development in Sub Saharan Africa: An Agenda for Action*, Washington, DC: World Bank.

Urban Bias Revisited: Staple Food Pricing in Tanzania

DEBORAH FAHY BRYCESON

This article examines the impact of staple food price controls on the Tanzanian urban and rural population during the 1970s and 1980s. It is argued that the objective of government pricing policy was spatial egalitarianism. Evidence of variable urban food consumption strategies, the agrarianisation of towns, the rise of parallel marketing and the slowing of urban growth casts doubt on the relevance of the urban bias concept to Tanzania and helps to explain the relative ease with which market liberalisation was introduced.

Over the past decade, much adjustment-related food policy has been premised on the assumption that the food pricing and marketing structures of African states have been oriented systematically toward favouring urban over rural inhabitants, and consumers over producers. The reversal of such 'urban bias' has therefore constituted a central objective of policy reform, not least in international programmes proposed to the Tanzanian government, which has often been cited as a primary example of a state promoting 'urban bias'.

This article rejects the notion of stark opposition between producers and consumers, and between rural and urban areas, and substitutes for the concept of 'urban bias' the alternative theme of spatial equality in food pricing. It can be argued that between 1973 and 1986 the pricing policy of the Tanzanian government with respect to maize, the main staple food, represented an attempt to achieve spatial egalitarianism, affording consumers relatively equal access and producers equal rewards. The rationale for this, its viability and inherent paradoxes, and the extent to which equality was indeed promoted, particularly given the insistence of international

Deborah Fahy Bryceson, African Studies Center, Leiden. The author is grateful to William Baynit for his research assistance and to Cynthia Hewitt de Alcántara for her helpful comments on the first draft of this article. For a more detailed discussion of food pricing and marketing reform in Tanzania, see Deborah Fahy Bryceson, *Liberalizing Tanzania's Food Trade: Public and Private Faces of Urban Marketing Policy, 1939–1988*, prepared for the UNRISD research programme on adjustment-related food policy.

monetary institutions on market reform, are examined in the following pages.

After discussing the significance of national integration and spatial egalitarianism in the post-colonial political economy of Tanzania, the evolution of food pricing and marketing policy is evaluated in terms of its effects on rural–rural, urban–urban and rural–urban equality. Related socio-economic and demographic change, specifically with respect to urban growth, is also observed in light of preliminary 1988 census results and findings of the author's 1988 food supply survey among urban households. Finally, in reviewing the policy debate between the Tanzanian government and international lending institutions, the extraordinary gap between the real course of development in urban and rural areas, on the one hand, and the terms of that debate on the other, can be highlighted.

REDUCING DIFFERENCES AND MEETING BASIC NEEDS

By African standards, Tanzania is a relatively large country, with extreme ecological and ethnic diversity. Over 100 different African tribal groupings populate the country in addition to a small Asian community and minute numbers of Europeans. During the colonial period, Tanganyika, as it was then called, was ruled on the basis of a three-tiered racial hierarchy: the vast majority of Africans were peasants, Asians were traders and Europeans were administrators. The post-colonial government, formed under the direction of the Tanganyika African Nationalist Union and Nyerere, its leading figure, was not surprisingly bent on securing political and economic power for the African majority. Unlike many other post-independence governments, however, it took precautionary measures against the creation of an African ethnic hierarchy based on regionalism.

The danger of regional conflict existed. A north–south divide had surfaced during the colonial period due to the lack of transport and infrastructural investment in the south. Peasant cash crop production developed in the central and northern parts of the country, and the prevalence of a cash economy in the north contrasted with the largely peasant subsistence character of production in the south. The post-independence government therefore pursued the objective of national integration and the lessening of regional inequalities. Rashidi Kawawa, a southerner and a Muslim, became prime minister, offsetting the presence of President Nyerere, a Christian from a small tribe in the north.

The importance of equitable regional economic development was reflected in the Second Five Year Plan (1969–74), which aimed at distributing industrial investment outside Dar es Salaam in nine regional towns to assure 'even' growth. Furthermore, in 1972 the government inaugurated a policy of administrative descentralisation, reorganising and rationalising government planning and financial expenditure in all twenty regions of Tanzania, under the aegis of regional and district development directors and their teams of functional officers. Although civil servants in Dar es Salaam were loath to be transferred to the regions, the government sent them there anyway, apparently in the belief that the presence of high-ranking officials could promote faster development of the rural areas.

Since emphasis was placed on rapid development, there was an attendant need for generous financial endowment. Regional Integrated Development Planning (RIDEP) exercises were initiated to attract support from foreign donors. During the latter half of the 1970s each of the 20 regions was subjected to the scrutiny of expatriate planning teams sponsored by different donor agencies, with implementation of the plans ultimately depending upon whether or not the donor agencies offered funding. In fact, only a few regions received substantial financial support, and the earlier growth pole strategy made even less impact on regional development because it could count on little follow-up financing.

Despite the fact that such conscientious efforts on the part of the government to promote national integration through regional development policies had relatively little impact [*Kleemeier, 1982: 49–50*], a second and less heralded area of public policy, concerned with food pricing, did indeed have a profound influence on national economic integration. This was, ironically, the case even though the primary concern of food pricing policy was to address economic welfare at the household level, rather than to provide equal development opportunities throughout the national territory.

Food pricing policy in Tanzania incorporated a basic needs approach long before 1967, when Nyerere officially declared the Tanzanian government's intention to build socialism. Throughout recorded history, the country had been threatened by the sporadic incidence of famine [*Bryceson, 1990*]. British colonial food policy attempted to deal with this threat by declaring the principle of peasant household self-sufficiency in food. During times of rural famine, district food self-sufficiency was advocated together with government famine relief and the suppression of food trade; and during the Second World War, when urban food shortages were experienced, food price controls and rationing were introduced.

Since national independence in 1961 coincided with a widespread famine, it is therefore not surprising that the newly-installed independent government moved in the direction of food marketing control. The National Agricultural Products Board (NAPB), founded in 1963, not only regulated the market for basic products, but over the longer term was intended to offer infrastructural support for the spread of African marketing co-operatives and to encourage the displacement of Asian produce traders.[1]

On average, Tanzanian dietary intake is based heavily on cereals and starchy roots. Maize is the most important staple food, accounting for roughly half of total urban calorie consumption and approximately 60 per cent of national consumption. The most widely eaten staple dish consists of ground maize flour called *sembe* cooked into a stiff *ugali* porridge. The post-colonial government's egalitarian objectives with respect to food pricing therefore centred on maize. Rice, wheat and root crops were of secondary concern in official food policy, and the prices of these crops tended more closely to reflect true production and transport costs.

The idea of encouraging spatial egalitarianism through ensuring that producers throughout the country would receive the same price for their maize was put forward during the early 1970s, at a time when the government was taking decisive steps to restructure agriculture and industry along socialist lines. Whether the theme of egalitarianism in Tanzanian pricing policy should be attributed entirely to the declared policy of socialism or whether egalitarian values associated with traditional acephalous tribal structures continued to influence public morality is a debatable point outside the scope of this article.[2] In any case, spatial egalitarianism was a central goal of food pricing policies during the 1970s and 1980s, as the following sections will indicate.

MAIZE PRICING AND RURAL–RURAL EQUALITY

For the Tanzanian state, 1973 was a year of heady optimism. It was the year that the nationwide campaign to move the rural population into newly-created villages was launched, as well as the year that the NAPB was disbanded and the urban-based state milling complex, called the National Milling Corporation (NMC), was elevated to the status of single-channel state marketing agent for staple foodstuffs. These changes arose out of official dissatisfaction with the marketing performance of the NAPB and co-operatives, as well as out of a preoccupation with achieving food security and ensuring stable producer and consumer prices.

The National Milling Corporation was obliged to move away from previous pricing policy, in which co-operatives had paid farmers a residual amount after deducting transport and handling costs from a set into-store price, and to buy all maize offered to it throughout the country at a standard pan-territorial price. Thus for the first time in the history of Tanzania, all maize producers could expect to receive the same price, no matter where they were located. This policy was of course extremely expensive and constituted a serious financial drain on the resources of the NMC. It took no account of the cost of transporting goods from remote regions over an extremely skeletal road and rail network, at a time when the development of transportation infrastructure in fact had lower priority than support for other budgetary categories like social services. But the 'straw that broke the camel's back' came in the form of two drastic oil price increases in 1973 and 1979, which caused transport costs to soar.

Under the pan-territorial pricing arrangement, rapid and dramatic change occurred in the regional pattern of official marketed production. While previously most marketed grain had come from the northern and central parts of the country, it was the south that blossomed during the 1970s. Following implementation of pan-territorial pricing, Ruvuma, Rukwa, Iringa and Mbeya regions quickly moved to the fore in commercial maize production and constituted a dynamic force within an economy otherwise plagued by declining production.

Although development of agricultural production in the south was an important accomplishment, it was overshadowed by problems arising from the enormous increase in transport costs required to sustain it. The capital city of Dar es Salaam, on the coast, was the major centre of food demand; and pan-territorial pricing served to encourage the geographical specialisation of marketed food production in a way exactly opposite to that which would have minimised transport costs from centres of maize production to the capital. The most distant areas from Dar es Salaam, namely Ruvuma, Rukwa, Iringa and Mbeya, were producing the greatest amounts of officially marketed food crops. These regions, which came to be known as the 'Big Four', accounted for only 17 per cent of national maize purchases in 1973/74, but 87 per cent in 1981/82 (Table 1).

The World Bank and other aid agencies heavily criticised the expense of pan-territorial pricing and invoked the principle of comparative advantage, which led the government to revise the policy, but not in the direction that economists hoped for. From 1982 until 1988, producer prices were based on the principle of climatic comparative advantage. Those regions climatically suited to maize growing were given a premium price, and it happened that Ruvuma, Rukwa and Mbeya were extremely well suited to maize production in terms of climate and soils. Hence the NMC's transport costs were increased, not decreased. Policy-makers justified the step on the grounds that NMC transport costs would be reduced, since it would no longer have to be prepared to purchase maize in all 20 regions of the country. By narrowing maize specialisation to fewer regions, it was hoped that costs would decline. This did not prove to be true.

The extreme reluctance of the government to abandon this pricing policy was related to the fact that most national policy-makers, and especially those from the southern regions, considered the integration of the latter into the national economy to be a major achievement of the post-independence

TABLE 1

NMC/COOPERATIVES MAIZE PURCHASES, 1973/74–1987/88

('000 Tonnes)

Year	National Tonnage ('000)	Regional (%) Coast/DSM	Morogoro	Tanga	Kilimanjaro	Arusha	Mara	Shinyanga	Mwanza	Kagera
1973/4	73.8	0	7	0	8	9	8	0	1	0
1974/5	23.9	0	4	13	20	12	7	0	0	0
1975/6	91.1	2	12	22	5	11	1	1	3	0
1976/7	127.5	2	7	16	5	12	5	0	1	1
1977/8	213.2	1	7	3	11	28	3	1	1	1
1978/9	220.4	0	2	3	6	32	2	1	2	0
1979/80	161.1	0	1	0	4	29	2	1	1	0
1980/1	82.8	0	1	0	0	20	0	0	0	0
1981/2	89.4	0	0	2	0	4	0	0	0	0
1982/3	86.0	0	0	3	1	1	0	0	0	0
1983/4	71.0	0	0	1	0	9	2	0	0	1
1984/5	89.5	0	1	3	0	3	0	0	0	0
1985/6	178.5	0	0	0	0	20	0	2	3	0
1986/7	172.8	0	0	2	0	27	0	2	1	1
1987/8	229.4	0	1	0	1	31	1	0	1	0

Year	Kigoma	Tabora	Singida	Dodoma	Lindi	Mtwara	Iringa	Mbeya	Rukwa	Ruvuma	'Big Four'[1]
1973/4	0	0	2	47	0	0	15	2	0	0	17
1974/5	0	3	0	0	0	0	17	3	3	18	41
1975/6	0	3	1	7	1	3	12	2	3	14	31
1976/7	1	9	1	9	2	3	12	4	9	8	33
1977/8	0	4	0	8	1	1	10	5	4	8	27
1978/9	0	2	2	17	1	0	12	3	2	10	27
1979/80	0	10	0	17	0	0	16	4	10	11	41
1980/1	0	3	1	3	0	0	26	6	22	17	71
1981/2	0	1	0	5	0	0	37	8	18	24	87
1982/3	0	2	0	2	1	0	30	11	21	26	88
1983/4	0	0	0	7	0	0	35	11	14	18	78
1984/5	0	0	0	1	0	0	26	8	19	38	91
1985/6	0	1	3	7	0	0	21	9	16	16	62
1986/7	1	1	3	4	0	0	21	7	16	13	57
1987/8	0	0	4	11	0	0	28	6	8	7	49

Source: Marketing Development Bureau [*1988*].
1. Iringa, Mbeya, Rukwa and Ruvuma combined.

government. Removing the transport subsidy would have constituted a form of betrayal. In 1989, however, the National Milling Corporation was directed to reduce its purchases by 50 per cent and to operate on a strictly commercial basis, buying only from the regions where it was cost-effective to do so. According to first hand observers' reports,[3] maize producers have since complained of being abandoned by the government in those regions; and disillusionment with commercial maize growing has reached a point at which many of the younger farmers entertain the idea of returning to the cultivation of traditional millet.

MAIZE PRICING AND URBAN–URBAN EGALITARIANISM

The issue of spatial egalitarianism in maize pricing for urban consumers poses an apparent paradox, which will be explored in the following pages before going on to consider questions of balance between entitlement and access to food in urban and rural areas.

Until the Second World War, the urban population of Tanzania was extremely small. Growth of Dar es Salaam and the major regional capitals began during the war, expanded in the 1950s, and accelerated after independence (Table 2). The history of state intervention in food marketing is closely linked with urban development, and with attempts to protect the urban population from food shortage and inflation. Thus in conjunction with colonial food price controls and rationing during the Second World War [*Bryceson, 1987: 169–70*], government civil servants received a cost of living allowance to compensate for the effects of inflation on stagnant salaries, and African civil servants' cost of living allowance included food payments.

As during the 1940s, the 1970s and early 1980s constituted a period of rapid inflation amidst government efforts to hold the wage and salary levels of public servants down; and it was in such a context that Robert Bates noted the extremely low prices at which the National Milling Corporation supplied urban consumers in Tanzania with their staple food needs [*Bates, 1981: 38–9*]. Over the years, this urban bias increasingly evolved toward what might be seen as urban *capital* bias, as the government protected the residents of Dar es Salaam at the expense of distribution to other regions. By 1983/84, 70 per cent of NMC *sembe* sales took place in Dar es Salaam and 30 per cent in the regions, whereas in 1974/75 these figures had been reversed.

This suggests that the principle of spatial egalitarianism was ultimately *not* pursued on an urban–urban basis. In view of the Tanzanian government's stated egalitarian objectives, it is surprising that the inequitable distribution of officially marketed maize and the privileged position of Dar es Salaam consumers did not engender public protest on the part of urban dwellers in other regions. Certainly such policy contradicted official attempts of the

TABLE 2
TANZANIAN URBAN CENSUS TOTALS

	Urban Settlement <20,000	% of National Population in urban Settlement <20,000	Dar es Salaam	Mwanza	Mbeya	Arusha	Songea
1988 Population	2,464,273	10.9	1,117,334	156,908	116,069	77,092	46,955
pgr[1]	4.1		3.8	3.6	4.2	3.4	10.1
1978 Population	1,655,167	9.7	769,445	110,553	76,601	55,223	17,955
pgr	10.4		9.9	11.2	18.1	5.1	11.5
1967 Population	557,750	4.7	272,515	34,396	12,325	32,012	5,430
pgr	12.8		7.8	5.7	5.9	12.3	14.5
1957 Population	166,795	1.9	128,742	19,877	6,932	10,038	1,401

Source: National population censuses 1957, 1967, 1978 and 1988.
1 pgr – population growth rate

kind just described, to promote a more even pattern of urban development in the various regions of the country, as well as the concomitant desire to avoid the over-development of Dar es Salaam. Furthermore, the growth of a national parallel market in maize, related to the failure of the National Milling Corporation to supply food to upcountry towns, was at odds with the concern of the government for national integration.

It is clear that the NMC, headquartered in Dar es Salaam, was stretched to the limit in the task of buying and transporting marketed output to the capital during the 1970s [Bryceson, 1985b: 61–8]. The distribution of grain to all parts of the country was therefore beyond the physical, managerial and logistical capability of the organisation. At the same time, a more decentralised produce buying and distribution network would have been impossible to coordinate, given the lack of efficiency of the NMC as well as the many difficulties of transport. In any case, after 1979 domestic procurement by the NMC declined, initially as an outgrowth of the transport shortage caused by the Ugandan war, and then because of drought and the spread of parallel maize marketing. The provisioning capacity of the Corporation was premised increasingly on imported maize. Dar es Salaam was the port where maize was off-loaded, and given the city's large staple food demand, imported stocks not surprisingly tended to stay in the capital.

In addition, demand for maize seems to have been outstripping supply between 1973 and 1985 throughout the country as a whole: the data presented in Tables 1 and 3 show high responsiveness of maize prices to variations in domestic supply. Under the circumstances, urban food shortages were frequent, not only in Dar es Salaam but also in several regional urban centres.

How was the relatively favoured position of Dar es Salaam in distribution justified in view of the egalitarian stance of the government? The short answer to this question is that such favouritism was neither justified nor publicised. Presumably, the view of policy-makers was that it would not become a public issue, which in fact it did not. Still, there were many politically powerful government and party figures resident in regional towns. Did they simply acquiesce to discriminatory pricing? In terms of populist politics, was it simply that the political clout of Dar es Salaam residents, the largest concentration of educated and economically powerful individuals in the Tanzanian citizenry, was so much greater than people living in the upcountry towns? In a nationwide speech in 1979 Nyerere did admit that 'Sugar and sembe [shortages] bothered him most especially in DSM [Dar es Salaam], which was very different from places like Musoma.[5] The shortage of the two items in DSM caused quite a stir' [Daily News, 16/12/79]. This quotation seems to support the notion that Dar es Salaam residents had a stronger political voice. Nevertheless, it is worth exploring

TABLE 3

MAIZE RETAIL PRICES: (Tsh./Kg)

		Open Market:				
	Official	Dar es Salaam	Mwanza	Mbeya	Arusha	Songea
1982/83[1]	3.35	6.86	6.62	4.41	3.88	2.92
1983/84	4.39	-	11.82	11.96	12.73	3.81
1984/85	5.40	6.16	16.79	6.90	16.36	4.53
1985/86	7.60	13.75	11.58	8.56	10.69	5.33
1986/87	12.20	14.59	9.60	8.73	11.59	6.22
1987/88	12.20	18.06	17.45	13.10	17.18	8.50
1988/89[2]	17.00	17.48	20.09	13.60	16.54	8.40
Weighted Mean	8.52	13.46	14.03	9.56	12.87	5.60

Source: Marketing Development Bureau [*1988*].

1. Nov. 1982–June 1983
2. July–Dec. 1988

the possibility that there is something more to be read into the phrase 'DSM is a very different place from Musoma' or other upcountry towns.

This can be accomplished in part through reference to data from a survey of 188 households carried out by the author in November 1988, for the purpose of exploring differences in food supply in Dar es Salaam and four upcountry towns: Mwanza, Arusha, Mbeya and Songea. Population totals and inter-censal growth rates for these urban areas have already been listed in Table 2, and a brief description of each will be provided below.

Dar es Salaam's large population relative to other towns and its natural harbour have contributed to its dominance as Tanzania's commercial capital throughout the twentieth century. Officially, the political capital of Tanzania was moved from Dar es Salaam to Dodoma during the 1970s, but in practice, Dar es Salaam has continued to function as the seat of national government due to its superior infrastructure and its metropolitan status.

Mwanza is Tanzania's second largest city with a population of almost a quarter of a million people at the time of the 1988 census. Situated on the shores of Lake Victoria, it has been a centre of (often illicit) trade between Tanzania, Kenya and Uganda. The railroad, which has connected Mwanza with Dar es Salaam since 1928, facilitated the growth of the former as a cotton entrepot. Its agricultural hinterland has, however, long been a maize deficit area, due both to its climate and to specialisation in cotton production on the part of the peasantry. Surpluses of rice are produced and exported from the area in good harvest years.

Arusha, half the size of Mwanza, is Tanzania's ninth largest town. Its hinterland is a grain surplus area, producing maize as well as wheat; and until 1980, maize sales to the National Milling Corporation from Arusha were in excess of most other regions. Drought and the increasing prevalence of parallel markets in grain have caused this to change, although a recovery of official maize sales was experienced in the late 1980s. Coffee plantations occupy much of the immediate hinterland surrounding Arusha town.

Mbeya, ranking fourth in the urban hierarchy, is in an enviable position in two respects. Situated in the Southern Highlands, where rainfall is high and relatively reliable, food harvests tend to be less erratic than those in many other parts of the country. Agricultural land is extremely fertile and produces surpluses of maize, rice and bananas. At the same time, Mbeya enjoys extremely good transport connections, since it is located on the TanZam Highway and near the Tazara railway, which connects the Zambian copper belt with the harbour at Dar es Salaam.

Songea, down the scale at fifteenth place in the urban hierarchy, is located in the extreme south. Though relatively small, it has recently experienced a great growth spurt associated with the construction of a tarmac road through the Southern Highlands [*Airey et al., 1989*]. Songea's hinterland is a major maize-producing region that benefitted substantially from pan-territorial pricing.

Table 3 shows the nationwide official retail price for maize as well as retail prices for maize on the parallel market in each of these towns between 1982/83 and 1988/89. Averaging the prices over time suggests that Songea residents were availed the cheapest supply of parallel-marketed maize at a very low TShs. 5.60/kg. Dar es Salaam residents with access to official maize retail prices were in the second most favoured position, paying TShs. 8.52/kg. It should be noted, however, that the number of Dar es Salaam consumers with ready access to officially marketed supplies was shrinking over time. Mbeya's parallel market offered relatively reasonable maize prices at TShs. 9.56, whereas average parallel market prices for Arusha and Dar es Salaam respectively were TShs. 12.87 and 13.46, peaking in Mwanza at TShs. 14.03.

Thus during most of the 1980s, residents of Dar es Salaam did not necessarily enjoy a large advantage in maize procurement. Songea residents had access to cheaper maize than inhabitants of the capital who could buy at the official price; and the parallel market price in Dar es Salaam was among the highest in the sample. In addition, results from the 1988 household survey suggest that households in the upcountry towns were somewhat *less dependent* on food purchase than Dar es Salaam residents (Table 4). In the upcountry towns there was in fact a distinctly higher incidence of direct urban household farming. The relatively smaller size of all upcountry towns in comparison with Dar es Salaam affords a greater possibility of farming on the perimeter of the town or even in sizeable gardens attached to the house. Furthermore, the potential of Dar es Salaam's agricultural hinterland is poor relative to that of the other towns with the possible exception of Mwanza. The climate and soils of the coastal belt are not suited to grain production.

Returning to the question of why 'urban capital bias' in official food distribution has been tolerated by up-country urban dwellers, one working proposition is that in Tanzania, where the vast majority of the urban population is made up of first generation urban dwellers and an urban life-style is not deeply entrenched, any expenditure on food is considered a

TABLE 4

SOURCES OF HOUSEHOLD FOOD SUPPLY

(Per cent)

Source	Dar es Salaam	Mwanza	Mbeya	Arusha	Songea
Purchased	88.8	79.1	62.2	79.3	36.1
Farmed by Household	5.2	15.2	30.1	12.2	62.7
Transfers from Relations & Friends	6.0	5.0	7.5	8.3	1.2

Source: 1988 Author's Household Survey.

hardship, since most people are used to own-farm household supplies. The fact that residents of upcountry towns have better access to direct farm supplies puts them at a comparative advantage relative to people living in Dar es Salaam. In the case of Mwanza and Arusha the margin of difference is not very great, but it could none the less help to cushion against food price fluctuation.

Thus in the eyes of the public, notably urban residents in upcountry towns, the priority that the National Milling Corporation has given to supplying Dar es Salaam could be considered as more of a compensatory measure than a manifestation of bias. Spatial egalitarianism in consumer maize prices between towns has not been achieved, but evidence from the household survey suggests that an approximation of spatial egalitarianism in food access may prevail. It should perhaps be emphasised that this is often equality of deprivation, not of sufficiency.

MAIZE AND RURAL–URBAN EQUALITY

Most of the criticism of staple food pricing in Tanzania during the early 1980s was from the perspective of urban bias [*Bates, 1981: 119–32; Ellis, 1982*]. It is important to note, however, that at that time, official pricing policy was in fact weighted more favourably towards producers than towards consumers.[6] Between 1973 and 1983 maize producer prices rose, and then returned to their 1973 level in real terms, while the decline in wage earners' purchasing power from 1975 onwards outweighed the effects of subsidized *sembe* prices for consumers (Table 5).

The period of greatest subsidy for *sembe* ran from 1979 to 1984, as the government attempted to compensate for the relentless drop in real wages. In 1980, this subsidy provided real benefits to low-income workers; but during the next few years it managed only to keep the purchasing power of the minimum wage (measured in kilogrammes of *sembe*) propped at 20 per cent below its 1973 level. Finally, with the complete removal of the consumer subsidy in 1984, official maize prices rose drastically in Dar es Salaam. This did not entirely eliminate the gap between official and parallel market prices, however, because some elements of subsidy remained in official operations, and parallel market prices reflected the higher costs of domestically produced maize, transported over land, as opposed to cheaper imported maize supplies shipped to Dar es Salaam and directed by the NMC to the Dar es Salaam market (Table 3).

The massive increase in maize consumer prices in conjunction with general inflation took its toll on real wages. By 1988, the minimum wage was worth only 24 per cent of its 1973 value or 29 per cent when measured in terms of the quantity of maize which could be purchased at the official price.

TABLE 5

COMPARISON OF REAL AND NOMINAL MAIZE PRICES FOR RURAL AND URBAN AREAS

| | RURAL: | | | URBAN: | | | | | | Purchasing Power | |
| | Producer Prices: | | | Sembe Consumer Prices: | | | Minimum Wages: | | | in Kg Sembe per: | |
Year	Nominal	Constant[1]	Index[2]	Nominal	Constant[1]	Index	Nominal	Constant[1]	Index[1]	Day's Nominal Wage	Index
1973	.33	8.38	100	0.80	22.99	100	240	6888	100	10.0	100
1974	.55	11.36	136	1.25	29.21	127	340	7937	115	9.1	91
1975	.80	14.24	170	1.25	25.15	109	380	7646	111	10.1	101
1976	.80	13.04	156	1.75	32.29	140	380	7002	102	7.2	72
1977	.85	12.42	148	1.75	28.93	126	380	6276	91	7.2	72
1978	.85	10.70	128	1.75	24.93	108	380	5409	79	7.2	72
1979	1.00	9.87	118	1.75	19.51	85	380	4237	62	7.2	72
1980	1.00	7.82	93	1.25	11.05	48	480	4244	62	12.8	128
1981	1.50	9.41	112	2.50	17.73	77	600	4252	62	8.0	80
1982	1.75	8.19	98	2.50	13.23	58	600	3174	46	8.0	80
1983	2.20	8.50	101	2.50	10.92	48	600	2620	38	8.0	80
1984	4.00	11.10	132	8.00	25.11	109	810	2542	37	3.4	34
1985	5.25	11.25	134	13.75	33.31	145	810	1961	28	2.0	20
1986	6.30	10.38	124	13.42[3]	25.00[3]	109[3]	1053	1961	28	2.6[3]	26
1987	8.20	10.25	122	13.42[3]	20.00[3]	87[3]	1260	1876	27	3.1[3]	31
1988	9.00	9.00	107	18.70[3]	18.70[3]	81[3]	1644	1644	24	2.9[3]	29

Source: compiled from Marketing Development Bureau figures [1988].

  1. Basis for calculation is 1988.
  2. 1973 = 100.
  3. Maize grain (*sembe* flour no longer sold in official market). In *sembe* milling, approximately 10% of grain is lost. The *sembe* price equivalent for maize grain is calculated at 110% of the official maize grain price.

Thus the level of consumer maize prices seemed to imply urban unsus-tainability rather than urban bias. Such a dramatic decline in urban purchasing power is especially striking when compared to the bouyant real producer price index for maize, which fluctuated between over 70 per cent and under seven per cent of its 1973 level (Table 5).

As the distribution of subsidised maize shrank geographically to Dar es Salaam, spatial equalisation of food access was undermined not only on an urban–urban basis, but also on an urban–rural basis. The vast majority of peasant households in the rural areas grew their own food. The fulfillment of their staple food requirements was comparatively unproblematic. Peasant households were in a favoured position, growing their own maize and retaining sufficient amounts for their household consumption needs. In bad harvest years, such as 1983/84, they might refrain from selling any of their maize output. In the urban areas, on the other hand, the decline in official maize purchases between 1980/81 and 1985/86 caused food shortages and escalating prices in the open market (Tables 1 and 3).

Provisional data from the 1988 census suggests that the deteriorating urban food supply situation during the 1980s could have had a depressing effect on overall urban population growth [*Tanzania, Bureau of Statistics, 1989*]. Between 1967 and 1978 urban growth was exceedingly high, averag-ing 9.1 per cent per annum for Dar es Salaam and the 18 regional capital towns listed in Table 6. In contrast, the inter-censal growth rate between 1978 and 1988 was less than half that, at 4.1 per cent per annum.

Figure 1 is a scatter plot of each town's average maize consumer price during 1982–88 relative to the percentage increase in the size of its popula-tion between 1978 and 1988. As expected, town population increase is negatively correlated with average maize prices. The r^2 is low, but significant at the 0.05 confidence level.

Although the effect of extreme values sheds doubt on the robustness of this finding, Figure I none the less reveals some interesting patterns. Songea stands out as the town with the most rapid urban growth and the lowest maize prices. Its extremely large positive growth residual is more than likely associated with the new tarmac road, completed in the early 1980s, which connects Songea to the national road grid, as well as with relatively favourable terms of access to maize. Sumbawanga (Rukwa region), Mbeya and Iringa, representing the other three major southern commercial maize growing areas, are easily identifiable as a cluster, experiencing above average urban growth, but lower than expected in relation to maize con-sumer prices (Table 6 and Figure 1). This might be explained by the commercial food crop boom experienced in these areas. Agriculture provided an attractive alternative to urban migration for the rural youth of these regions.

TABLE 6

AVERAGE MAIZE CONSUMER PRICES, NOVEMBER 1982–DECEMBER 1988 AND
INTER-CENSAL POPULATION GROWTH RATES BY TOWN

Town	Official Price	Average Maize Consumer Price[1]	Population Growth: Census 1988[3]	Census 1978	% Increase	Growth Rates: 1978-88	1967-78	% Change
Arusha	8.52	12.87	77,092	55,223	39.6	3.4	5.1	-33
Bukoba	8.52	14.65	28,702	21,547	33.2	2.9	9.3	-69
Dar es Salaam	8.52	10.99[2]	1,117,334	769,445	45.2	3.8	9.9	-62
Dodoma	8.52	12.00	74,677	45,807	63.0	5.0	6.3	-21
Iringa	8.52	9.99	84,860	57,164	48.5	4.0	9.3	-57
Kigoma	8.52	12.10	51,719	50,075	3.3	0.3	8.2	-96
Lindi	8.52	10.50	41,587	27,312	52.3	4.3	6.9	-38
Mbeya	8.52	9.56	116,069	76,601	51.5	4.2	18.1	-77
Morogoro	8.52	13.03	102,986	60,782	69.4	5.4	8.4	-36
Moshi	8.52	11.72	96,838	52,046	86.1	6.4	6.8	-7
Mtwara	8.52	13.71	76,632	48,491	58.0	4.7	8.3	-43
Musoma	8.52	13.76	63,652	31,051	105.0	7.4	6.6	12
Mwanza	8.52	14.03	156,908	110,553	41.9	3.6	11.2	-68
Shinyanga	8.52	13.14	18,056	20,439	-13.2	-1.2	13.4	-109
Singida	8.52	9.96	39,598	29,258	35.3	3.1	10.8	-71
Songea	8.52	5.60	46,955	17,955	161.5	10.1	11.5	-12
Sumbawanga	8.52	7.27	47,878	28,586	67.5	5.3	n.a.	-
Tabora	8.52	9.82	92,779	67,388	37.7	3.3	11.2	-71
Tanga	8.52	12.61	129,951	103,399	25.8	2.3	5.1	-55
AVERAGE/TOTAL	8.52	11.44	2,464,273	1,673,122	47.3	4.1	9.1	-55

1. Except in the case of Dar es Salaam, average maize consumer prices are equated with the Marketing Development Bureau's published open market prices which are the monthly averages of recordings of maize grain retail prices collected by Ministry of Agriculture personnel on the 1st and 15th of each month in town markets throughout the country. The prices are given in TShs. per debe which is a volume measurement roughly equal to 17 kgs.
2. Assumes that 50% of supplies are derived from the official market and 50% from the open market. Dar es Salaam's average open market price during the period under review was TSh.13.46/Kg.
3. Provisional census urban ward totals of urban districts. It should be noted that the urban totals are subject to future revision due to reclassification of rural and urban boundaries. Any revision of the classification of urban and rural wards in urban districts is likely to give higher urban totals, but it is not anticipated that the increase would exceed an overall urban growth rate of 5.5%.

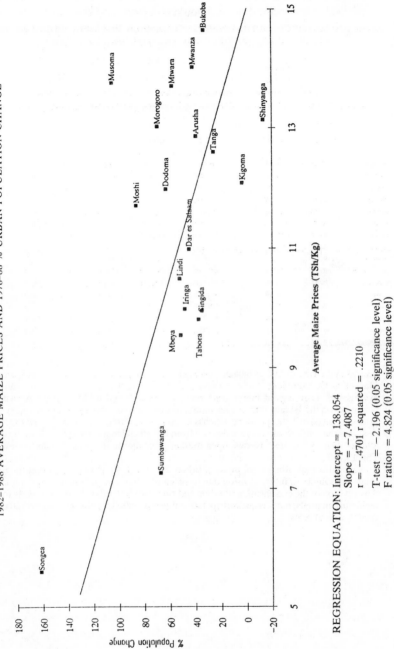

FIGURE 1

1982–1988 AVERAGE MAIZE PRICES AND 1978–88 % URBAN POPULATION CHANGE

REGRESSION EQUATION: Intercept = 138.054
                                    Slope = –7.4087
                                    r = – .4701 r squared = .2210

                                    T-test = –2.196 (0.05 significance level)
                                    F ration = 4.824 (0.05 significance level)

In contrast, the three Lake Victoria port towns of Bukoba, Mwanza and Musoma, which are located in maize deficit regions and register the highest consumer maize prices, have below average growth (Table 6) but slightly positive growth residuals (Figure 1) in the two former cases and an extremely large positive residual in the latter case. Since these are towns which have traditionally been entrepots for both legal and illicit trade with Kenya and Uganda, their growth could be heavily influenced by external trade. This would make them less subject to the economic constraints facing urban residents in other parts of the country.

'MARKET LIBERALISATION': LOCAL–NATIONAL–INTERNATIONAL PRICE CONVERGENCE

In the context of its socialist development strategy, the goal of the Tanzanian government was to establish a comprehensive state marketing system for food crops that offered spatially equitable prices to producers and affordable prices to consumers. However, the state marketing system was not monolithic and regional government administrations varied in the extent to which they enforced price controls and tried to check the growth of parallel markets. The fact that the Ministry of Agriculture itself collected parallel market maize price data from 1982 onwards constitutes a strong indication that parallel markets were a significant economic phenomenon and that Tanzanian state market controls were neither comprehensive nor fully implemented. Despite Tanzania's image abroad as a zealous socialist country with all-embracing statist policies, pragmatism in policy formulation and a willingness to scrap policies in the face of obstacles were features of the post-independence government, almost to the point of trial-and-error experimentation.

The operational inadequacies of state marketing were glaring, and the state marketing system was pressured to reform both from above and from below. Peasant farmers and urban consumers expressed their dissatisfaction with the system through participation as buyers and sellers in parallel markets. At the same time, international agencies led by the IMF and World Bank were concerned with the disincentive effects on producers of poor marketing services and low prices. The worsening deficit position of the National Milling Corporation, implying a serious drain on national finances and general inflationary effects within the economy, also prompted IMF demands for reform.

Strained relations between the IMF and the Tanzanian government prevented the signing of a loan agreement between the two parties from 1980 to 1986. President Nyerere's speech to the foreign diplomatic corps, on New Year's Day of 1980, headlined 'NO to IMF Meddling', publicly announced the rift [*Daily News, 3/1/80*]. According to one author, the IMF responded with stiffer conditionality 'to teach Tanzania a lesson' [*Wangwe, 1987: 153*]; see also Biermann and Campbell, [*1989*]. The major bone of contention was the government's refusal to massively devalue the Tanzanian shilling.

Concern among bilateral donors about Tanzania's failure to come to terms with the IMF lay behind significantly reduced external assistance. Successive national programmes were then mounted with names that spelled out their objectives: the National Economic Survival Programme [NESP] (1981–82), the Structural Adjustment Programme [SAP] (1982–85) and the Economic Recovery Programme [ERP] (1986–89). NESP was an overambitious drive to increase national production and exports within the framework of the existing economy. It was soon recognised to be inadequate. Under the Structural Adjustment Programme which followed, many of the demands of the IMF were addressed, although not always to the stipulated degree. A series of small devaluations was implemented; parastatal reform was pursued in connection with an overall pruning of the central budget; and in order to ease consumer shortages and the government's severe foreign exchange constraints, import controls were lifted in 1987 to allow own-funded imports by Tanzanian residents. Furthermore, a 'development levy' or head tax was imposed on all adults.

The 1984 national budget marked a turning point with respect to the organisation of grain marketing. Not only was the consumer subsidy on *sembe* removed, causing its official price to treble, but district road blocks designed to check 'black marketing' of grain were removed, and private individuals were allowed legally to transport up to 500 kilograms per lot.

Despite these reforms, which were implemented immediately, negotiations with the IMF continued to be deadlocked until 1986. By that time, Nyerere had stepped down from the presidency and his successor, Mwinyi, was eager to pursue more drastic economic liberalisation. Prices were then decontrolled on all but twelve essential items, and a step-like series of devaluations finally won Tanzania the seal of approval of the IMF.

In 1987, all restrictions on the transport and movement of food grain by private traders were lifted, although traders were still not permitted to buy from peasants or co-operative societies. Their purchases were technically restricted to the National Milling Corporation and the co-operative unions. Inter-regional transport rates were also deregulated; and following the recommendations of a high-level Task Force which investigated food pricing and distribution in 1987, steps were taken to delimit the role of the NMC and to stop further escalation of its deficit. This brought about the closure of a number of NMC branches in the regions, staff retrenchment and the setting of volume ceilings for purchases in 1988. Furthermore, through the enforcement of ceilings on bank credit to co-operative unions, those unions which were heavily endebted were refused the necessary finance for crop purchase; and this in effect further restricted official sources of grain supply.

A chronicle of *formal* pricing and marketing reforms nevertheless provides an extremely partial picture of developments in the Tanzanian grain market. Whatever pressure was exerted by the IMF and international donor agencies for market reform was secondary to the pressure exerted by the actual existence and spread of local parallel marketing from 1979 onwards.

While it is impossible to know the volume handled in local parallel markets, or the rate of growth of that volume over time, it is clear that the breakdown of grain purchasing by the NMC during the 1979 Ugandan war, associated with lack of transport, cemented the foundations of extensive 'black marketing' in grain in the north and encouraged the flow of maize from Arusha and Kilimanjaro to the deficit regions of Mwanza and Shinyanga. Several authors have hazarded guesses, based on fieldwork, about the importance of parallel markets in specific localities [*Loft and Oldevelt, 1981: 96; Odegaard, 1983: 18–30; Rasmussen, 1985: 8–14*]. Thus the Marketing Development Bureau estimated in 1984 that 75 per cent of all marketed maize went through parallel markets [*Tanzania, Marketing Development Bureau, 1984*], although in view of the severe transport constraint throughout the country at this time (brought on by petrol shortages, lack of spare parts and unmaintained roads), 75 per cent seems exceptionally high. By 1988, the Bureau's estimate was down to 64 per cent [*Tanzania, Marketing Development Bureau, 1988*].

In the author's 1988 household survey of Arusha, Mwanza, Dar es Salaam, Mbeya and Songea, respondents reported that virtually all purchases of maize were made in the open market, even in Dar es Salaam. This growing reliance on the higher-priced open market maize seems to have been a gradual process. It is thus important to note that from the perspective of the urban household, 'market liberalisation' did not take place as a result of any sudden policy change. On the contrary, official market reform apparently confirmed an already existing state of affairs, coming in a very real sense 'after the fact' of shifting household provisioning strategies.

More pertinent to the urban household than a mere official acknowledge-ment of the status quo, government market reform was a legitimation of household economic activity. Preliminary findings from the five-town trader survey which accompanied the 1988 household survey indicate that large numbers of people started trading during the economically depressed 1980s as a survival strategy, to weather the escalating prices associated with economic crisis. Many took up trade as a secondary source of income which often proved more lucrative than their 'official' employment. Others used redundancy payments from factory and parastatal staff layoffs as the starting capital for their trading activities. Still other strategies involved having one family member in trade, notably the wife, while other members of the household dedicated themselves to wage employment. Although the official market reform did not provide credit or infrastructure for pursuing trading activities, it did reduce the risks that these newly established traders faced, removing the threat of government confiscation of their assets (as in previous anti-trader campaigns) and giving them confidence to pursue trade openly.

Given this information, it becomes easier to understand why, unlike Zambia, Tanzania did not experience popular unrest following changes in government policy to conform to IMF conditionality. The removal of the 1984 *sembe* consumer subsidy and the various reforms that followed caused little consumer protest. Biermann and Campbell attribute this to 'the role played by the Party (CCM) in depoliticising the population' [*1989: 79*]. While this may be true in part, and subsequent party-organised protest against the IMF[7] suggests that the party did act as a forum for venting complaints, it is none the less unlikely that the party could have suppressed the protest of massive numbers of people across the wide spectrum adversely affected by the economic liberalisation programme of the government. If the impact of market liberalisation had been *too* adverse, political protest could not have been avoided. It therefore seems more likely that the lack of widespread or violent political protest resulted as much from a combination of factors originating in the nature of urban Tanzanian households as from features of economic or political organisation at the level of the nation state.

In the first place, it should be noted that the impact on urban households of price inflation and substantial increases in consumer maize prices preceded government market reforms by a number of years, as the influence of parallel markets spread. Worsening shortages of officially marketed *sembe* during the early 1980s in fact weaned urban dwellers away from dependence on the subsidy before the latter was officially abolished [*Bryceson, 1985a*]. Thus inflation was gradual and household adjustment to it as 'a fact of life' was incremental.

Second, Tanzanian urban households had at their disposal a range of behavioural patterns which might be considered their own forms of 'structural adjustment'. Given the overwhelmingly agrarian nature of the national economy and society, the recent immigrant status of urban dwellers and the small size of most up-country towns, many households could switch to growing a portion of their own staple foods. Alternatively, vegetables and other foodstuffs could be grown to sell for additional income. In addition, the close ties of kinship between urban and rural branches of the extended family made it possible for some urban residents to depend partially on food transfers from rural relations. At the same time, many urban households adjusted to inflationary food costs by becoming traders themselves. In this context, market reform had mixed connotations, offering economic opportunity as well as posing the threat of household immiseration.

Finally, it must not be overlooked that for many urban households, notably those living in up-country towns, the parallel market was often their only source of marketed maize supply. Under the circumstances, urban residents had to recognise their dependency on parallel markets and were generally appreciative of their existence in the absence of official supply. However, consumers were often critical of parallel market prices and of various aspects of parallel market operations linked in part to their uncertain legal status. Under the circumstances, market liberalisation was greeted with relief, on the assumption that in future parallel market supplies would not be threatened by preventative measures on the part of the government and that certain aspects of open market operations and infrastructure could then be improved.

CONCLUSION

In summary, the Tanzanian government's pre-reform attempt to achieve spatial egalitarianism by offering producers throughout the country uniform maize prices and affording consumers roughly equal access to staple food supplies was, in effect, largely successful in political terms. Assessing the situation prior to the IMF agreement, it is evident that, with respect to rural–rural equality, pan-territorial maize producer prices managed to integrate the southern regions into the national economy. On an urban–urban basis, it appears that urban access to staple food supply was sufficient to prevent urban political unrest. In rural–urban terms, political evaluation is more difficult. Rural–urban terms of trade, which were considered heavily biased towards the urban areas during the 1970s, fell drastically against the urban areas during the 1980s. Rural–urban levelling was taking place to the point that the division of labour between the two was no longer very distinct.

From an economic perspective, the objectives, policies and policy implementation of spatial egalitarianism were riddled with contradictions and high costs, and in the long run proved unsustainable. Localised parallel markets and IMF pressure served gradually to undermine official programmes which were intended to create spatial egalitarianism in food pricing; and the 1986 agreement between the Tanzanian government and the IMF signified at least a temporary end of the experiment.

As a result of adjustment-related policy reforms, southern maize-producing regions are no longer availed pan-territorial producer pricing, thereby jeopardising the advances of the preceding decade with respect to rural-rural egalitarianism. A total elimination of southern participation in the national market is not, however, likely in view of the better rail and road infrastructure gained by the southern regions during the 1980s.

With respect to urban-urban inequality, the removal of the *sembe* subsidy and the elimination of the 'urban capital bias' undoubtedly has made Dar es Salaam households more vulnerable to food insecurity than those in any other part of the country. Given the size of the city, the average resident of Dar es Salaam does not have the same degree of manoeuvrability as residents of more agrarian-based upcountry towns, much less those of rural villages. The increased vulnerability of large numbers of people in the capital to food insecurity, like the decrease in support for maize farming in southern provinces, may have political implications which are yet to become visible.

It is worth noting in conclusion that no matter how much international and market pressures may have been at odds with government policy throughout Tanzania's experiment with spatial egalitarianism, household coping strategies in fact appeared to converge with the objectives of the government. At an aggregate level, the impact of Tanzanian household coping mechanisms was to level urban and rural differences, as urban households took to farming or relying on rural relations for supply. Furthermore, urban migration rates and urban population growth decreased to a moderate rate in comparison with the exceptionally high rates of the 1970s.

It is undoubtedly not accidental, given the majority of the population living in rural areas and the rural origins of most urban dwellers, that an agrarian outlook and values strongly influenced urban households' coping mechanisms and, it could be argued, served as the philosophical basis for the government's egalitarian objectives as well. Ironically, as official pricing policies became less and less viable, the cumulative impact of agrarian-based household strategies was to achieve egalitarianism between producers and consumers and between rural and urban areas. Unfortunately, however, the levelling process proceded in a direction which was exactly the opposite of that which the government had hoped to promote. Standards of living and household food security are on the decline, especially in the urban areas, as urban dwellers level down.

Given the real course of development of the maize provisioning structures in Tanzania, it seems almost surrealistic that throughout the first half of the 1980s food policy debate revolved around whether an open market was 'to be or not to be', while vast numbers of Tanzanian householders knew that it already existed and were not uncommonly participants in it as buyers, sellers or traders. The sharp distinctions drawn between producers and consumers, as discrete individuals, were often equally unreal, since urban householders were frequently producers as well as consumers. Even the distinction between urban and rural populations was, in the face of urban crisis and urban–rural ties, considerably overemphasised.

As long as economic crisis conditions prevail, and projections for the 1990s do not inspire optimism, it is likely that spatial egalitarianism, as an organising principle of Tanzanian political economy, will persist, more as a concomitant of decentralised household decision-making than as an outgrowth of state policies. But if present trends continue, intra- and inter-household transfers will be restricted to equalising deprivation, not opportunity.

NOTES

1. For a more detailed analysis of colonial and post-colonial marketing policy see Bryceson [1992].
2. For a discussion of this, see Bryceson [1992: Ch.1].
3. Personal communication from a Rukwa regional historian, Professor Marcia Wright of Columbia University.
4. Millet is Rukwa's traditional staple food crop, and has commercial value for beer brewing.
5. Musoma is a town on the shores of Lake Victoria and the regional capital of Mara, Nyerere's home region.
6. In a subsequent article, Ellis revised his opinion [Ellis, 1984].
7. In November and December 1988, following the Tanzanian government's agreement with the IMF on the second phase of the Structural Adjustment Programme and an additional 20 per cent devaluation, both Temeke and Kinondoni district party leaderships in Dar es Salaam region held public meetings to let the people voice their opposition. Most of the opposition took the form of complaints about inflation [Daily News, 3/12/88].

REFERENCES

Airey, T., Bryceson, D. and J. Howe, 1989, 'Interim Evaluation of the Songea-Makambako Road', Overseas Development Administration, UK.
Bates, R.H., 1981, Markets and States in Tropical Africa, Berkeley, CA: University of California Press.
Biermann, W. and J. Campbell, 1989, 'The Chronology of Crisis in Tanzania, 1974–86', in B. Onimode (ed.), The IMF, the World Bank and the African Debt: The Economic Impact, London: Zed Books.
Bryceson, D.F., 1985a, 'Food and Urban Purchasing Power: The Case of Dar es Salaam, Tanzania', African Affairs, Vol.84, No.337, pp.517–21.
Bryceson, D.F., 1985b, 'The Organization of Tanzanian Grain Marketing: Switching Roles of the Co-operative and the Parastatal', in K. Arhin, P. Hesp and L. van der Laan (eds.), Marketing Boards in Tropical Africa, London: KPI.
Bryceson, D.F., 1987, 'A Century of Food Supply in Dar es Salaam: From Sumptuous Suppers for a Sultan to Maize Meal for a Million', in J. Guyer (ed.), Feeding African Cities, Manchester: Manchester University Press.

Bryceson, D.F., 1990, *Food Insecurity and the Social Division of Labour in Tanzania, 1919–1985*, London: Macmillan.

Bryceson, D.F., 1993, *Liberalizing Tanzania's Food Trade: Public and Private Faces of Urban Marketing Policy, 1939–1988*, London: James Currey/UNRISD.

Daily News, 16/12/79, 'Mwalimu on Food Situation: No Need to Panic'.

Daily News, 3/1/80, 'Mwalimu's New Year Message: NO to IMF Meddling'.

Daily News, 3/12/88, 'Temeke Queries IMF Ties'.

Ellis, F., 1982, 'Agricultural Price Policy in Tanzania', *World Development*, Vol. 10, No. 4, pp. 263–83.

Ellis, F., 1984, 'Relative Agricultural Prices and the Urban Bias Model: A Comparative Analysis of Tanzania and Fiji', *Journal of Development Studies*, Vol. 20, No. 3.

Kleemeier, L., 1982, 'Foreign Assistance Projects in Regional Planning, Tanzania 1972–1982', Geography Department seminar paper, Dar es Salaam: University of Dar es Salaam.

Loft, M. and J. Oldevelt, 1981, *Developments in Peasant Agriculture in Kigoma Region during the Post-Villagisation Years*, Economics Research Bureau.

Odegaard, K., 1983, 'An Analysis of the Food Market in a Dual Market Structure: The Case of Maize in Tanzania', Arne Ryde Symposium, University of Lund, Sweden, Aug. 1983.

Rasmussen, T., 1985, *The Private Market for Maize in Tanzania: A Preliminary Analysis*, Copenhagen: Centre for Development Research Paper D.85.13.

Tanzania, Bureau of Statistics, 1989, *1988 Population Census: Preliminary Report*, Dar es Salaam: Ministry of Finance, Economic Affairs and Planning.

Tanzania, Marketing Development Bureau, 1984, *Price Policy Recommendations, I*, Dar es Salaam: Ministry of Agriculture.

Tanzania, Marketing Development Bureau, 1988, *Annual Review of Maize, Rice and Wheat*, Dar es Salaam: Ministry of Agriculture.

Wangwe, S.M., 1987, 'Impact of the IMF/World Bank Philosophy: The Case of Tanzania', in K. Havnevik (ed.), *The IMF and the World Bank in Africa: Conditionality, Impact and Alternatives*, Uppsala: Scandinavian Institute of African Studies.

The Political Economy of Food Pricing and Marketing Reforms in Nicaragua, 1984–87

PETER UTTING

This article examines the process of food policy reform in Nicaragua during the mid-1980s and asks why a government of 'socialist orientation' embarked on the adjustment path. The author argues that policy changes favouring liberalisation should not be seen simply as a pragmatic top-down response to economic crisis but rather as an accommodation on the part of the state to a new balance of social forces and state–society relations.

Most analysts of economic reform in Third World socialist societies tend to explain the reform process as a pragmatic response on the part of the post-revolutionary state to a set of critical economic and/or socio-political conditions. Problems of an economic/technocratic nature are likely to receive particular attention: stagnant or declining production levels, macro-economic disequilibria, sectoral imbalances, reduced levels of surplus appropriation by the state, waste and microeconomic inefficiency, low labour productivity. Socio-political issues associated with regime legitimacy, social discontent and the question of ideological rifts within the party leadership may also be considered.

All these factors are likely to be relevant. To understand the reform process fully, however, it is important to look more closely at the process of social change underlying the creation and later transformation of Third World socialist experiments: changes occurring in social structure, involving

Peter Utting, United Nations Research Institute for Social Development. This article draws upon a study carried out within the context of the research programme on adjustment-related food policy of the United Nations Research Institute for Social Development. Field work was financed in part by the International Development Research Centre of Canada. The Nicaraguan experience was compared with that of three other Third World socialist countries for a doctoral dissertation at the University of Essex, later published as *Economic Reform and Third-World Socialism* (London: Macmillan, 1992).

the emergence or growth of specific social groups; developments at the level of civil society where workers, producers, professionals, women, consumers and other groups associate, organise, articulate interests and form pressure groups; and finally, changes taking place in participatory processes and practices, as different social groups gain or lose capacity to influence policy design and implementation. From this perspective, radical policy reform becomes not simply a pragmatic top–down governmental exercise but an accomodation on the part of the state to a new balance of social forces and state–society relations.

PROBLEMS OF REVOLUTIONARY TRANSFORMATION IN NICARAGUA

Following the overthrow of the Somoza regime in July, 1979, the Sandinista government embarked on an ambitious programme of reconstruction and development intended to transform what has been called a 'repressive agro-export' economy [*IFAD, 1980*]. Under Somoza, investment had been concentrated in activities associated with the production, processing and export of cotton, coffee, beef, sugar and bananas. During three decades, the fruits of economic growth were largely concentrated in the hands of a small landed elite and bypassed both agricultural labourers and the peasantry – groups which constituted over half the national population and lived in extreme poverty.

Patterns of resource allocation promoted by the *Somocista* state had also done little to support the significant group of small commercial farmers, with access to sizeable tracts of land in the interior, who produced some agro-export crops and beef. Pricing policy as well as restrictions on access to bank credit, infrastructure and agricultural support services tended to discriminate against these 'rich peasants' and hinder their transformation into capitalist producers.

The pre-revolutionary agro-export model generated intense migratory processes and rapid urbanisation. At the time of the revolution, nearly 30 per cent of the population lived in Managua alone. Reflecting the relatively limited industrialisation of the country, and the small size of its working class, the bulk of all urban residents were engaged in so-called informal sector activities. Thus from the middle of the twentieth century onward, the food system of Nicaragua was increasingly shaped by the needs of the capital for large quantities of staple foodstuffs, as well as for imported non-essential food products consumed by a growing middle class. Cheap food for the urban masses was guaranteed through a highly exploitative set of social relations, often involving tied loans from local moneylenders, which left the mass of basic grain producers selling part of their crop for little return.

The process of revolutionary transformation set in motion in 1979 attempted to induce rapid improvement in the living conditions of low income groups and to modernise the Nicaraguan economy through agricultural technification, agro-industrial expansion and the development of energy infrastructure. The model of development which first emerged, however, was characterised by a number of imbalances or biases. There was a tendency to privilege 'state-centred accumulation' [*Kaimowitz, 1986*; *FitzGerald, 1989*], involving high rates of investment and priority in resource allocation for the state enterprise sector (formed on the basis of confiscated *Somocista* properties). This was associated with patterns of 'urban-centred consumption' whereby certain basic needs programmes primarily benefitted urban residents.

The Limits to Planning

The ambitious investment programme launched by the Sandinista government occurred within a context of centralised planning, which was favoured over more decentralised planning methods or reliance on macroeconomic policy instruments to maximise resource mobilisation and promote the 'rational' use of available resources. Nevertheless, a combination of structural, material and technical conditions rendered central planning highly problematic.

Following the confiscation of *Somocista* property, the revolutionary state found itself in direct control of only a fifth of the agricultural sector and a third of industry. These sectors of the economy were still largely in private hands and contained an important element of petty-commodity production. The highly atomised and dispersed character of production acted as a major structural constraint on planning. Furthermore, the very openness of the Nicaraguan economy and its dependence on foreign markets and aid restricted the capacity of the state to determine import levels accurately and to control the price system [*FitzGerald, 1986: 34*].

The institutional organisation of the state apparatus also impeded planning [*Bernales, 1985*]. The economic power of the state was, in effect, highly diffused among a number of key ministries which in certain respects tended to operate independently of one another, although their respective areas of economic activity were closely articulated. The creation of a variety of separate institutions and state-run service enterprises caused particular problems in the agricultural sector, where it complicated producers' access to essential goods and services.

Other more technical problems also impeded the planning effort. Following the revolution, there was a serious lack of information on the Nicaraguan economy – how it was structured, the complexity of production systems, the logic of different economic agents. Very often the data required to formulate policies and plans simply were not available. Moreover, when such information was forthcoming it was often 'overpoliticised', highlighting the importance of the state enterprise sector and private (capitalist) producers [*Baumeister, 1988a: 230*]. Relatively little was known about the large mass of small producers who tended to be bypassed by the state in certain areas of economic policy [*Baumeister, 1988a: 231; Kaimowitz, 1986: 100; Zalkin, 1988*].

In addition, certain forms of state intervention had the effect of disarticulating marketing circuits. Policies which displaced merchants, for example, also ruptured traditional networks linking rural and urban markets, thereby affecting the flow of food products to the towns as well as the availability of manufactured goods or processed food products in rural areas [*CIERA, 1987*]. At the same time, decisions regarding the use of foreign exchange tended to prioritise 'heavy' producer goods, mass or urban consumption goods (food, medicines, etc.) and general agricultural inputs such as fertiliser, pesticides and seed, without recognising the importance of so-called 'peasant goods' such as imported *machetes*, maize grinders, rubber boots, and so forth, on which small producers depended. Since many of these goods were obtained from other countries in the region, their acquisition was also affected by the collapse of the Central American Common Market during the first half of the 1980s.

State-Centred Accumulation Bias

Production inputs and investment resources were concentrated largely in state agricultural and agro-industrial enterprises, which were considered the engine of growth for the economy. This had the effect of 'crowding out' individual peasant and capitalist producers in the structure of resource allocation [*FitzGerald, 1988a: 18*]. In consequence, state enterprises assumed somewhat of an enclave character, with limited links to other forms of property and farming systems. Such a situation contrasted sharply with the pre-revolutionary model in which large landowners performed a series of functions which, while involving exploitative relations, provided informal credit, certain inputs, transport and consumption goods required by peasant households.

While the performance (in terms of output) of state agricultural enterprises compared favourably with that of other forms of production, the former incurred significant financial losses. In 1983, these were cancelled by the government; but within two years, the state sector had again accumulated major debts. When a second bailout was approved, an increasing number of policy makers questioned the feasibility of a state-centred accumulation model [*Biondi-Morra, 1988: 2*].

Meanwhile, as more and more resources were channelled towards large-scale projects, the tension between accumulation and consumption increased. A planning imbalance favouring accumulation over consumption had emerged clearly as early as 1982, when resources were increasingly concentrated in relatively large and often slow-yielding development projects and when investment accounted for 21 per cent of GDP. Financing such projects added to inflationary pressures. The public investment programme, while overly ambitious to start with, was to become unsustainable when the country was at war and subject to the types of economic boycott measures outlined below.

War and Economic Boycott

Attempts by the Sandinista government to address the underlying causes of poverty and underdevelopment involved a struggle to transform the historical pattern of insertion of Nicaragua in the world economy – more specifically, a struggle against the traditional forms of economic and geopolitical domination of the United States in the Central American region. The economic, military and diplomatic response of the United States government was to have a devastating effect on the economy.

The war seriously undermined agricultural production. Co-operatives and rural infrastructure were damaged, trade circuits disarticulated, peasant stocks depleted and labour redirected toward the military. In many areas agricultural production either reverted to a subsistence regime or was abandoned altogether. An estimated 16 per cent of all farming land in the three interior regions of the country (Regions I, V, VI) eventually fell into this latter category [*DGFCDC, 1988c*].

It is important to stress that such conditions not only restricted production and reduced marketed surplus but also acted as a brake on the the the expansion of the agrarian frontier which, historically, had been an important factor underlying increases in production of key products such as maize, beans, cattle, coffee, and lumber [*Baumeister, 1988a*].

At the national level, the effects of the war greatly contributed to the macroeconomic disequilibria that became a prominent feature of the Nicaraguan economy from 1983 onward. By the end of 1985, the total cost of the conflict (direct costs plus indirect effects) amounted to approximately two billion dollars (more than the entire GDP for one year) [*Marchetti and Jerez, 1988*]. Material destruction, combined with production and other losses attributable to the trade embargo imposed by the United States government in May 1985, created a drop in export revenue equal to approximately one-third of total export earnings during the 1983–85 period.

The rapid increase in defence expenditures from 1983 onwards also generated pressures on current accounts. Allocations for defence and security increased from 19.7 per cent of total government expenditure in 1983 to 32.2 per cent in 1985 [*Delgado, 1986*]. The extremely large fiscal deficit sustained from 1983 onwards contributed in turn to a rapid increase in the money supply and to inflationary pressures.

The diversion of wage goods and other resources towards defence activities had major implications for agricultural and industrial production, as well as for the level of living of the civilian population. For example, supplying the armed forces with boots and uniforms accounted for 45 and 24 per cent of manufacturing capacity of the the shoe and textile industries, respectively, while army food supplies represented ten per cent of national consumption in 1984 [*FitzGerald, 1987: 207*]

Following the suspension of bilateral assistance, the Reagan administration pressured for an end to loans from multilateral lending agencies such as the World Bank and the Inter-American Development Bank [*Barraclough et al., 1988*]; and by the end of 1985, an estimated 273 million dollars in loans had been withheld. The economic boycott further served to distort the economy. Increasing reliance on socialist bloc assistance meant less flexibility in determining the composition of imports, as well as reduced foreign exchange liquidity and shortages of vital inputs and spare parts for the production of essential goods [*FitzGerald, 1988b: 317*]. In addition, as foreign credits from multilateral agencies were reduced, it was increasingly necessary to finance the fiscal deficit through monetary emission. This constituted another important element in the inflationary pressures which built up between 1983 and 1986.

Response of Social Groups to the Process of Transformation

Levels of production, productivity, state procurement and investment were also undermined to some extent by responses on the part of various social groups to programmes and policies which sought to transform social relations and structures of income and wealth.

Particularly important in this respect was the response of the *agrarian bourgeoisie* to a situation in which it retained ownership of a significant share of the means of production but was deprived of political power and effective control of investment [*FitzGerald, 1985*]. Moreover, although the process of land expropriation proceeded slowly, certain producers, notably extensive cattle ranchers, felt that property rights were threatened by the agrarian reform.

Between 1982–83 and 1984–85, agricultural production fell sharply in crop sectors such as rice, coffee, cotton, and sugar cane, where this kind of producer played an important role. Not only did volume of output decline, but also the share of total production accounted for by this group. Investment was seriously affected. In the agricultural and agro-industrial sector, the percentage of total accumulation accounted for by large-scale private enterprise fell from 21.3 to 15.1 per cent between 1980–82 and 1984–85 [*Kleiterp, 1988: 19*].

State procurement of food for domestic provisioning, raw materials for local processing plants and agro-export products was affected not only by declining production but also by the fact that as the gap between official and black market prices widened, large producers sold increasing quantities of products like rice, sorghum, milk and beef through 'clandestine' channels. Idle capacity in many processing plants increased, and important by-products (notably those associated with beef processing) were also lost. In addition, an overvalued currency prompted many producers of such goods as beef and coffee to restrict export sales and supply the domestic market instead.

It is difficult, however, to generalise about the behaviour of capitalist producers. As Núñez shows, the sector became increasingly divided between the so-called 'cordoba' or 'patriotic' bourgeoisie, on the one hand, and the 'dollar' bourgeoisie, for whom decapitalisation and non-co-operation constituted not simply a rational response to an unfavourable economic climate but part of a more explicit political strategy to destabilise the economy and regime [*O. Núñez, 1987: 178*]. Much of the former group continued to engage in production and many medium-sized farmers associated themselves with the pro-Sandinista agricultural producers' organisation, known as UNAG.

Certain strategies adopted by *peasant producers* also contributed to the crisis. Particularly important in this respect was their tendency to reduce marketed grain sales and to withhold labour from the harvests. For rich peasant producers, as well as producers organised in co-operatives, the reduction in grain production and sales reflected the trend towards more diversified cropping patterns which emerged during the early 1980s, notably the shift toward more profitable cash crops [*Zalkin, 1985; 1987*]. Labour shortages also played a role in decisions by producers to restrict grain production [*Dore, 1988*]. Finally, some farmers preferred to buy heavily subsidised grain from the state provisioning agency (ENABAS) rather than producing it to feed their workforce. These trends intensified toward the middle of the 1980s, as relative prices shifted against grains [*Utting, 1987: 133*].

During this latter period, many rich peasants also sought to bypass state marketing channels and sell grain, coffee and livestock on the black or 'grey' market. Poor and middle peasants were simultaneously providing a smaller volume of marketed maize and beans, in part because the elimination of pre-revolutionary tenancy, credit and exchange relations reduced their obligations to deliver significant quantities of maize as payment to landlords, money lenders and merchants [*Dore, 1988; Utting, 1987: 133*].

Many peasant producers also refrained from selling their labour, particularly during the harvest period. The combination of declining real wages, improved access to land and credit (which increased the subsistence capacity of peasant households), shortages of consumers' and producers' goods, as well as fear of being recruited into the army, kept members of these households away from the harvest [*Enriquez, 1985*]. The replacement of traditional pickers by inexperienced urban youth, bureaucrats and workers was to have a damaging effect on productivity in the coffee plantations.

Labour productivity was also affected by a variety of strategies deployed by *industrial and agricultural workers*. The response among agricultural labourers to the relaxation of coercive labour relations, an austere government wage policy and shortages of both essential and non-essential goods was to work less, or less intensively. This was a rational reaction to the existing structure of incentives.

Government distribution policy clearly contributed to this problem. Many industrial workers spent an increasing proportion of their working day buying the cheap basic manufactured products to which they had access through a network of state supermarkets. Some of these products also found their way on to the black market [*Cabrales, Barricada, 14.11.87: 3*]. The phenomenon worsened during 1984 and 1985 when, in order to stem the flow of formal sector workers to informal sector activities and under pressure from the unions, many enterprises adopted a policy of paying a portion of workers' wages in kind. Much of this produce was subsequently sold on the black market, a turn of events which required that workers take considerable time off to engage in commercial activities.

Urban bias (reflected explicitly in the implementation of the food rationing and subsidy system which benefited mainly urban consumers) also contributed, in three important respects, to the deepening crisis. Concentrating resources in urban areas contributed to shortages of basic processed foods or manufactures in rural areas which, in turn, acted as a disincentive to peasant production and contributed to deterioration in the terms of trade from the point of view of the peasant producer. Second, relatively easy access to basic goods and services, as well as employment, combined with other policies such as that of allowing squatters to settle on vacant urban lots [*MIDINRA, 1984: 21*], attracted migrants to urban areas, and especially to the capital city. Third, the attempt rapidly to improve the social conditions of the mass of the population in urban areas implied very large budgetary outlays on social programmes and subsidies, which played a role in the fiscal deficit, monetary emission and inflation.

FOOD PRICING AND MARKETING REFORMS

Five years after the revolution, the country confronted a profound crisis. The gross domestic product, which had grown at an average of three per cent per year between 1981 and 1983, declined by two per cent in 1984–85. Export revenues dropped 40 per cent between 1981 and 1985. Inflation, which stood at 22 per cent in 1982, reached 334 per cent in 1985. Declining production of most major food products was reflected in falling per capita consumption. And significant instability in the employment structure prompted massive growth of the urban informal sector, which may have increased by as much as 66 per cent between 1983 and 1985. Concomitantly, there was a weakening of support for the revolutionary government, reflected in increasing local support for the *Contra* forces and the relatively poor showing of the Sandinistas in many rural areas in the 1984 elections.

While a number of significant economic and food policy policy changes were introduced in 1984, it was not until February 1985 that a comprehensive package of reform measures was announced. These were designed to contain growing macroeconomic disequilibria, boost agricultural production, curb parallel trading activities and the rapid growth of the urban 'informal' sector, and protect the levels of living of workers and peasants.

Specific measures included a reduction in subsidies, a freeze on government employment and expenditure levels in certain areas, the introduction of tighter controls on levels of public investment and the types of projects implemented, a 64 per cent devaluation of the Cordoba, significant increases in agricultural producer prices, productivity incentives for industrial and agricultural workers, considerable wage increases for the working class and state sector employees, the imposition of a number of controls on informal sector trading, as well as new taxes on merchants and self-employed professionals [*Pizarro, 1987*; *CIERA, 1984a*; *Avendaño, 1988*]. Throughout the remainder of 1985 and during the following two years additional measures were taken which not only extended many of these initiatives but also liberalised trade in certain food product sectors and introduced a system of selective provisioning of basic goods favouring workers and state employees over informal sector groups.

When taken together, such reforms mirrored both a change in development strategy and a shift in the pattern of alliances underlying the Sandinista regime. The goal of rapidly eliminating poverty and improving the levels of living of the mass of the population was replaced by one which sought to defend the levels of living of specific social groups, within the context of a 'survival economy' geared towards defence and toward the production and provision of certain essential goods and services. This new approach involved important changes in the pattern of resource allocation and implied granting new priority to rural areas, and most particularly to the peasantry.

Response to the needs of small agricultural producers, and to rural residents in general, is the hallmark of the set of food pricing and marketing reforms which will be briefly outlined below.

Altering the Domestic Terms of Trade

Immediately following the Sandinista victory, the revolutionary government radically transformed the marketing system for basic grains. Through ENABAS, the state-owned grain marketing board, the government intervened directly to control a significant share of national grain procurement and distribution, as well as all imports of maize, beans, rice and sorghum; and through the Ministry of Industry and Commerce, MICOIN, it set official producer prices, calculated on the basis of average production costs plus a stable mark-up.

During the early post-revolutionary period, the government also set retail prices for grains and other essential food and consumer products and instituted a large-scale programme of food subsidies. Through these policies, the state sought to stabilise producer prices, guarantee the supply of grains throughout the year, and maintain consumer prices low. In practice, however, this system acted as a disincentive to basic grain producers; and during the early 1980s, the domestic terms of trade clearly favoured urban consumers.

Beginning in 1984, measures were therefore introduced to shift the terms of trade in favour of agricultural producers. Changes in pricing policy altered the relative prices of basic grains and manufactures significantly: producer price increases for maize, beans and milk during the 1985–87 period were more than double those of certain basic manufactured products. This situation contrasted sharply with that of the previous period (1978–85), when price increases for articles such as clothing far outstripped those of food.

Liberalising Trade

Between 1980 and 1983, ENABAS had played an increasingly dominant role in the national grain market, increasing its purchases from approximately 180,000 metric tonnes in the former year to nearly 340,000 in the latter. ENABAS purchases of beans in 1983 accounted for approximately half of national production and 80 per cent of total marketed production; its purchases of maize in 1984 represented 27 per cent of the national crop and half of marketed production.

At the same time, a number of restrictions had been imposed on private traders, who could not move grain across district lines without authorisation and were only to buy and sell at official prices. Price controls, as well as a subsidy policy raising producer prices above the wholesale level, served to displace private merchants from the grain trade.

This situation began to change during the 1985–86 agricultural cycle, when there was a partial lifting of controls on private merchants in the three interior regions of the country where the atomised and dispersed character of bean and maize production, as well as war conditions, had prevented ENABAS from organising an effective procurement system. Intermediaries began to buy up maize and beans at approximately double the price paid by the state marketing agency, thus providing a clear stimulus to increased production.

To compete with private merchants, ENABAS not only announced significant price increases but also offered producers selling grain at its procurement depots the possibility of buying cheap manufactures. Regional governments were free, for the first time, to set their own official producer prices in response to local costs of production and market conditions; and state officials, in coordination with the main agricultural producers' organisation (UNAG), mounted community, municipal and regional as-semblies to encourage farmers to continue to sell a significant proportion of their surplus grain to ENABAS.

Moves towards liberalisation at this time were restricted to rural and regional markets. In an attempt to promote regional self-sufficiency and stem the flow of grains and other food products from the interior of the country to cities like Managua, roadside control posts were set up to prevent merchants or producers from shipping grain across regional boundaries. Given the unpopularity of this measure (even ordinary travellers on inter-city buses sometimes had certain provisions confiscated) and the difficulty of actually controlling inter-regional flows outside of official marketing chan-nels, these controls were eventually lifted in April 1987.

It proved similarly impossible to restrict the operations of private mer-chants in urban areas, although an attempt was made to do so for several years after the liberalisation of trade in rural settings. In the major cities, and particularly in Managua, the Ministry of Commerce only haltingly extended permission for private trade in grains. In fact, as it will be seen below, the government was extremely suspicious of small merchants and convinced of their role in bringing about unnecessary price increases for basic products. Therefore during 1985 and 1986 MICOIN in fact reduced the size of some urban market places, considered to constitute centres of speculative trading, and closed a number of others. Although licenses were issued to a certain number of urban traders, periodic police operations sought to remove illegal vendors from the main market places. Still, by 1987, some 40,000 traders or trading establishments, of a national total estimated to be of the order of 130,000, had been given official permits [*Cabrales, 1987*].

During that same year, the government adopted a new approach for dealing with intermediaries and informal sector traders. Instead of attempting to suppress their activities, an effort was made to integrate them into the 'formal' economy. Licenses were to be issued to another 40,000 traders, who would contribute to state revenues through both license fees and taxes. Regional governments sought to work with licensed merchants to organise the procurement of basic grains; and in the case of some regions, merchants were assigned specific procurement areas, notably those where ENABAS had a limited presence. These traders were encouraged to sell directly to retail outlets, in order to reduce the number of links in the commercial chain.

Rather than attempting to control all trade, government strategy thus moved toward selective intervention in areas of strategic importance for accumulation of commercial capital, notably the import trade and wholesale activities [*Cabrales, 1987*]. In the retail sector, the state eventually restricted itself to direct control of a network of supermarkets which expanded rapidly from the mid-1980s and numbered 36 in 1987. Furthermore, the state abandoned any pretension of controlling the marketing and distribution of all essential products and intervened primarily in those product sectors where experience had shown that effective control could be achieved, namely in sectors where production was concentrated in a few large-scale enterprises.

From Basic Needs to Selective Provisioning

These food pricing and marketing reforms involved a significant change in the broad basic needs approach characterising early post-revolutionary development strategy, which had identified 'popular sectors' in general as the intended beneficiaries of government social programmes, although in practice many programmes primarily benefitted the urban population. From the mid-1980s onward, the army and so-called 'productive sectors' (the working class and agricultural producers) were identified as priority groups, while state employees were placed at an intermediate level in the scale of priorities and the urban informal sector was relegated to last place.

A series of measures affecting the distribution of basic goods reflected this change in entitlements. In 1984, steps were taken to reduce the quota of basic products assigned to some of the more urbanised areas of the country, notably Managua, in order to increase allocations to regions in the interior, and particularly in the war zones [*CIERA, 1986*]. To take one example, the quantity of powdered milk assigned to the Managua area was reduced by a third in 1984 [*CIERA, 1984a*]. The government also radically reduced its commitment to supply the mass of the urban population with a wide range of essential consumer products [*Cabrales, 1987: 4*]. Between 1985 and 1987, the state attempted to supply the national network of official price stores (*expendios populares*) with only five basic products: sugar, vegetable oil, rice, soap and salt; but in practice it could not guarantee regular or sufficient supplies.

In contrast, the supply of designated 'peasant goods' (*machetes*, rubber boots, maize grinders, kerosene lamps and so forth) increased significantly in rural areas during this period. Through the Peasant Supply Programme, the Ministries of Agricultural Development and Agrarian Reform (MIDINRA) and Commerce and Industry (MICOIN) gave priority to providing 38 producer and consumer goods to rural areas.

The number of privately-owned rural retail outlets which operated as 'fair price shops' within the MICOIN system was expanded; and in addition, the concern of the Unión Nacional de Agricultores (UNAG) with the limited capacity of the state to supply rural areas prompted the organisation to involve itself directly in this task. Its work began in 1984 when an emergency programme, supported by the Swedish government and NGO aid, was implemented in a region where much of the peasant population had been affected by the war. By the end of 1987, approximately 200 peasant stores (organised mainly on a co-operative basis) were dotted throughout the country [*Serra, 1988: 33*].

Finally, subsidies on food products (grains, milk and sugar) which had primarily benefited the urban population were reduced or eliminated. In mid-1984, for example, the price differential on basic grains (which had kept official retail prices below producer prices) was eliminated, although the government continued to subsidise the administrative and operational costs of ENABAS. As a percentage of GDP, consumer subsidies on grains and milk fell from 3.8 to 0.5 per cent between 1984 and 1985 and were eventually eliminated in 1987 [*CIERA, 1989a*]. Sugar continued, however, to be subsidised during this period.

THE CHANGING BALANCE OF SOCIAL FORCES, PARTICIPATION AND THE POLICY PROCESS

To explain why major reforms in food policy were introduced during the mid-1980s, it is necessary to examine not only the nature of the economic and political crisis which enveloped the nation, but also developments at the level of civil society that served to restrict the 'relative autonomy' of the state, to alter the correlation of social forces and to modify the capacity of different groups to influence the process of policy design.

State–Society Relations

First, it is important to address the question of why the state originally assumed such a dominant role in rural society following the Revolution and why resources for production and investment were originally concentrated to such a degree in state enterprises, while the needs of important sectors of the peasantry were relegated to a secondary plane.

It is tempting to seek an easy answer to these questions by focussing on the issue of Sandinista ideology and noting the influence of orthodox positions within the technocracy and Party leadership, upholding the superiority of state enterprise and the need to encourage a process of forced modernisation/agro-industrialisation. Such perspectives clearly shaped the content of Sandinista development strategy [*Baumeister, 1988b: 5*], but they cannot in themselves explain the phenomenon of 'state-centredness'.

To do so we must refer also to three structural conditions existing both before and immediately after the seizure of state power by the Sandinistas. First, it must be recognised that even under Somoza, the Nicaraguan state had exercised a prominent role in the economy, acting as intermediary between the world market and national producers by creating favourable infrastructural conditions for agro-export producers [*O. Núñez, 1987: 43*], as well as providing more direct support for economic activities controlled by the Somoza group [*Weeks, 1988*].

Second, the insurrectionary process 'decapitated' rural society to some extent, removing certain elements of the local elite (particularly large landowners and merchants) from power. This created a vacuum which was not filled by other social groups, given a third structural condition of pre-revolutionary Nicaragua, namely the fact that the mass of the rural population did not constitute a cohesive social force. The Nicaraguan peasantry was highly dispersed, unorganised and not integrated to any significant degree in the revolutionary movement. When, by the late 1970s, the revolutionary struggle assumed a national dimension, it was the urban rather than the rural masses which actively engaged in the armed struggle to overthrow the Somoza dictatorship.

While rich peasant producers constituted, in quantitative terms, an important social group, their economic and political power had been restricted by the nature of the 'repressive agro-export' model. Certain fractions of the agrarian bourgeoisie had formed producer associations during the 1970s, but these remained elitist in character and did not attempt to incorporate smaller producers on any scale [*CIERA, 1989b*].

Thus the highly limited development of civil society in rural areas, as well as revolutionary changes in the rural power structure, created conditions in which the post-revolutionary state could freely exercise its 'relative autonomy'. Regional party officials, the bureaucracy and local managers of state enterprises stepped into a vacuum. Nationally, the state bureaucracy doubled in size during the early post-revolutionary period.

This balance of social forces helps explain both the 'state centredness' of the post-revolutionary development model and the urban bias which characterised certain government programmes. Not only did the urban masses make up the core of the insurrectionary movement, but during the pre-revolutionary period civil society was far more developed in urban areas than in rural ones. Relatively large sectors of the urban population were organised in trade unions, professional/political organisations, student associations, and so forth. Nearly a year before the seizure of state power by the Sandinistas, urban neighbourhood residents had in fact begun to organise in Civil Defence Committees [*CIERA, 1984b*]; and organisations such as these exerted a powerful influence on the policy process during the immediate post-revolutionary period. Moreover, the bureaucracy was highly concentrated in the capital, Managua.

The Emergence of the Peasantry as a Social Force

This correlation of urban/rural social forces, as well as of relations between the state and rural society, eventually underwent a number of major changes. One of the most significant political developments of the years leading up to the reforms concerned the growing strength of the organised peasantry.

During the immediate post-revolutionary period (1979–81), approximately 50,000 peasants and landless labourers were organised in agricultural co-operatives. There was at that time, however, no organisation which explicitly represented the interests of co-operative members and peasants, who together numbered some 150,000 families.

It was not until 1981 that the Sandinista party created the National Union of Farmers and Ranchers (UNAG). Its membership grew rapidly, however, reaching 125,000 by the end of 1986. Important changes also occurred in the social composition and demands of the organisation. Early demands and activities centred primarily on the development and consolidation of the co-operative movement and the recruitment of smaller producers. In 1984, however, following a change in the leadership, the UNAG began to recruit many commercial farmers – the so-called 'natural leaders' or 'patriotic producers' [*Luciak, 1987: 43*; *IHCA, 1989: 35*; *D. Núñez, 1989*].

While the general demands of the organisation, centring on issues associated with the land problem and improved access to basic goods, continued to favour co-operatives, and poor and middle peasants, demands associated more directly with larger producers or commercial farming interests came increasingly to the fore. These included issues associated with property rights (fear of expropriation and land invasions), access to capital goods and improved prices.

The drive to recruit medium- and large-scale producers also forced the members of co-operatives into a minority position within the organisation. Moreover, in practice, a significant number of the co-operatives originally set up as collectives were in fact operating as capitalist enterprises, attempting to maximise profits, capitalise their operations and employ wage labourers [*CIERA, 1985*]. Such developments had implications for the type of demands put forward by co-operative members.

That the interests of commercial farmers should be increasingly considered thus reflected not only the new level of organisation and bargaining strength of this group but also the impact of major structural changes associated with agrarian reform and agricultural development policy, which had transformed thousands of landless labourers and poor peasants into middle or rich peasants or members of co-operatives integrated into commodity markets [*Utting, 1988*].

As the UNAG grew in strength, it adopted a higher profile in politics. Throughout 1984, successive UNAG leaders demanded a far greater say in planning and economic policy decisions [*Torres and Coraggio, 1987: 200, 204*]. The president of UNAG came to preside over the agricultural commission of the National Assembly, which was influential in determining national agricultural policy [*Luciak, 1987: 49*]; and he participated in the National Planning Council, where major policy decisions were approved. UNAG representatives also sat on executive commissions concerned with the design, review and implementation of policies and plans associated with agrarian reform, credit, producer prices, taxes, the supply of basic inputs and consumer goods, production levels for coffee, cotton, beef, sugar and basic grains, as well as the provision of health and adult education services in rural areas [*Luciak, 1987: 49, 54; Wilson, 1987; IHCA, 1989: 38*).

Finally, UNAG participated actively in municipal councils, which played an important part in determining resource allocation and in proposing projects at the community level [*Wilson, 1987: 248*]. Regionalisation of the state planning and administrative apparatus clearly provided an institutional framework through which the UNAG could exert greater influence on the policy and planning process.

While the UNAG was closely linked to the FSLN and was generally supportive of the government, it nevertheless gained a reputation as an effective pressure group, channelling the demands of its membership upwards and getting results [*Vilas, 1986b: 29*]. Its leadership quickly developed an impressive capacity for consultation with members through local and regional assemblies. In 1984, such assemblies were held throughout the country; and through them, leaders came to understand the degree of discontent generated by shortages of essential inputs, implements and other goods [*Serra, 1988: 32*]. This process played an important role in decisions to increase the supply of work implements and basic consumer goods to rural areas.

During early 1986 local assemblies were again held throughout the country, culminating in April in the First National Peasant Congress, attended by some 500 peasant delegates and several top government leaders. The demands made by participants reinforced earlier reforms: particular stress was placed on the need for a more flexible approach to forms of co-operative organisation, greater support for individual producers and greater reassurance to larger producers, improved rural/urban terms of trade and rural supply systems, as well as a greater role for women in the peasant movement [*IHCA, 1989:37*]. What was noteworthy about the meeting was not only the extent to which government leaders endorsed the reform proposals but also the self-critical tone of several of the speeches by government leaders when evaluating state/peasant relations [*Wheelock, 1986*].

The Working Class: A New Alliance and a Specific Trade-Off

The abandonment of a 'cheap food' policy, which guaranteed urban workers' access to food at subsidised prices, clearly affected the level of living of the working class. Curiously, however, the two major organisations representing industrial and agricultural workers (the CST and ATC, respectively) accepted the policy changes with little opposition. Why did the main trade union organisations adopt this position?

In terms of numerical strength, they were not weak. The trade union movement had grown considerably following the revolution, from an estimated 27,000 workers before 1979 to 260,000 by mid-1986, or 56 per cent of the total number of wage-earners. By far the largest union organisation was the Sandinista confederation of industrial workers (CST), which claimed to represent 65 per cent of the total unionised labour force [*Vilas, 1986a: 12; 1986b: 28; Stahler-Sholk, 1986*].

Despite this growth in membership, however, the political strength of the CST declined. The latter tended to adopt the party line, which stressed the need for national unity, increased labour productivity, austerity and self-sacrifice, in order to win the war and create a 'survival economy'. In practice, this meant subordinating more economistic class demands which, in turn, weakened the base of support of the CST and resulted in tensions between the leadership and the rank-and-file [*Florez-Estrada and Lobo, 1986: 28–9*]. This situation particularly affected the CST, which had to compete with at least six other independent trade union organisations. The ATC, with a

virtual monopoly of the organisation of agricultural workers, proved somewhat more successful in combining or harmonising class and party demands
[*Florez-Estrada and Lobo, 1986: 29*; *Vilas, 1986b: 27*].

Trade union organisations were affected not only by adherence to the
party line, but by specific government controls which restricted certain
forms of pressure. Most important in this respect was the State of Economic
Emergency imposed in 1981, prohibiting strike action and demonstrations
[*Vilas, 1986a: 13*]. They were also influenced by an ideological shift,
involving a reconceptualisation (on the part both of party and union leaders)
of the nature of the class struggle. Attention turned away from the classic
antagonist of the working class - the industrial and agrarian bourgeoisie -
toward private commercial capital and unlicensed informal-sector traders,
who were seen to benefit from, and indeed to contribute to, the inflationary
spiral and thus to bleed the 'productive sectors' of the economy [*Vilas,
1986a*].

The identification of a new 'class enemy' coincided with a new definition
of the historical 'subject' of the revolution. In official Sandinista discourse,
less emphasis was eventually placed on the 'people' or the 'popular sectors'
in general and more stress on the notion of a worker-peasant alliance of
'productive' sector workers in general. Within this framework, the CST
recognised the need to give incentives to the peasantry to increase food
production and to tackle problems of inflation and shortages. It was nevertheless considered important that the benefits of increased production not
accrue to merchants and speculators. Hence the state would continue
to procure a portion of the harvests to supply both the working class and
the army and, in conjunction with mass organisations, would attempt to
clamp down on black market activities. This approach largely explains the
fact that trade liberalisation was restricted to rural and regional grain
markets during 1985 and 1986, while in the main urban centres the government at first continued to impose strict controls on the marketing of basic
products.

Explaining the response of the main union organisations to the change in
policy should not, however, be limited to consideration of state–union
relations and shifts in Sandinista ideology. Compensatory measures were
also taken by the government, which were themselves a product of working
class demands. Thus following the IV National Assembly of Trade Unions,
held in January 1985, an agreement was signed by the CST and MICOIN
under which workers and public sector employees would be given privileged
access to sixteen consumer goods. The products involved were primarily
basic manufactures such as clothes, footwear, kitchen utensils and batteries,
as well as a limited number of processed food products.

At the same time, an increasing number of state-run supermarkets in

Managua were converted into 'workers' supply centres' (CAT) where only workers (and family members) with union cards could shop. Such centres gradually appeared in other cities, while in smaller towns and in the countryside an increased supply of goods was delivered to commissaries located in the workplace.

Towards the end of 1985 assemblies held in over a thousand places of work, with more than 90,000 workers participating, culminated in a three day-national conference which placed issues associated with the supply of basic goods and price control next to defence as the top priority of delegates. Therefore during 1986 the network of CATs was expanded, increasing from three to seven in the capital alone, and the number of products sold through these outlets increased to 40. Certain food products, not contemplated in the original agreement, were also distributed through the CAT network [*MICOIN, 1987*]. In practice, however, quotas were often not met and real wages continued to decline.

By 1987 the government came under increasing pressure from the unions to change both its wage and basic goods provisioning policies. The practice of linking wages and salaries to inflation, which had operated for a short period between October 1984 and May 1985, was taken up again in 1987; but this time the decision was taken to link wages and salaries of formal sector workers to the increase in the cost of a basket of 54 products, the distribution of which was largely controlled by the state [*Ortega, Barricada, 7.6.87: 3*]. Like earlier attempts to protect the levels of consumption of the formal-sector working class, however, this experiment could not be sustained.

The Urban Informal Sector and the Sandinista Defence Committees (CDS): Declining Participation in the Policy Process

Of all mass organisations, the Sandinista Defence Committees (CDS), representing urban neighbourhood dwellers, participated most actively in the process of food policy design and implementation during the early 1980s. The rank and file membership of this organisation, which according to some estimates reached nearly 600 thousand [*CIERA, 1984b: 56*] (approximately half the population aged 20 and over), was composed to a large extent of urban residents whose incomes were linked to informal sector activities.

The CDS played a major role in establishing the guaranty card system, which was gradually expanded to provide family quotas for a number of essential food and non-food products. They were also influential in defining which type of retail outlets would constitute the basis of the official retail system. Pressure from the CDS, for example, influenced decisions to expand the territorial network of 'people's stores': small, privately-owned 'fair price shops' supplied in part through state-controlled wholesale companies, and distributing, along with other products, the basic goods sold on the guaranty card system. In addition, the CDS selected local retailers who could operate these 'people's stores' [*Utting, 1983*].

With the creation in 1983 of a high-level food policy review board (the National Supply Commission), the CDS were able to influence the nature of measures incorporated into the Consumer Protection Law, which was passed in July 1984 and subsequently reinforced in August 1985. The law increased the number of products to be included on the guaranty card system, nationalised wholesale distribution of 18 basic products and introduced a series of controls on marketing activities.

Once these measures were taken, however, the commission became less active and was eventually disbanded. While the rural and industrial workers' organisations continued to participate actively in the policy process, the participation of the CDS declined markedly. When the new National Planning Council was established as the highest planning authority of the government, in early 1985, the CDS were not asked to participate in an important commission overseeing production, prices, basic goods supply, salaries and employment, in which the CST and ATC were present.

The waning influence of the CDS in the policy process was to a certain extent symptomatic of an overall crisis affecting the organisation. Throughout 1984 and 1985, the active participation of community members in CDS activities, including those associated with overseeing the implementation of food pricing and distribution policy, declined sharply. Much of the urban population became critical of the organisation, which was seen to have divorced itself from real community interests and concerns and to be operating more as a parastatal organisation than in representation of its members.

The unhappiness of local people with the CDS deepened when the latter joined ranks with government agencies and the CST in 1984 in order to clamp down on unlicensed or illegal trading activities. Since many neighbourhood residents engaged in such activities, such policy alienated grassroots support. Moreover, the guaranty card system fell into disrepute when the so-called 'guaranteed' products distributed through the people's stores failed to arrive in the quantities required.

The informal sector, then, was squeezed not only economically, through the imposition of controls on commerical activities and cuts in certain social programmes, but also in terms of participation in the policy process itself, as exercised through the CDS. It was eventually 'squeezed' ideologically as well, as government rhetoric grew increasingly hostile to petty traders, and particularly to unlicensed merchants and street vendors. At times the 'antispeculator' rhetoric was employed to refer to a whole range of 'informal' activities.

The Bureaucracy: Inter- and Intra-Institutional Tensions

Finally, explaining changes in food pricing and marketing policy and state/peasant relations requires a brief review of a number of developments at the level of the state administrative and planning apparatus.

Within the Ministry of Agricultural Development and Agrarian Reform there were a number of divisions and top ministry personnel who supported the demands put forward by UNAG. From the early post-revolutionary period, the ministry had been divided along ideological lines between a technocratic faction which favoured concentrating resources in large-scale state enterprises and development projects, on the one hand, and a more pro-peasant fraction on the other. During the mid-1980s, the position of the latter was reinforced, not least because of the way the state-centred accumulation model had performed in practice.

Other tensions existed between the regional and central levels of the state bureaucracy. Administrative decentralisation, which was implemented from 1982 onward, increased the power of regional party and ministry delegates, who tended in general to be far more in tune with peasant demands than central-level officials.

A third area of bureaucratic conflict which became particularly apparent during the latter half of the 1980s was that between the 'production' or 'spending' ministries (notably Agriculture) and institutions concerned with state finance and external trade [FitzGerald, 1989]. Concerned with growing macroeconomic disequilibria, the latter pushed for an adjustment/ stabilisation package that involved a considerable freeing up of the price system, restrictions on state expenditures and changes in the sectoral allocation of resources.

Moreover, in an attempt to compensate for the decline in real incomes, an increasing number of public functionaries sought alternative employment, took on two jobs at once, moved from one state agency to another in search of slightly higher wages and engaged in quasi-legal or corrupt practices. Developments such as these clearly affected the capacity of the state to intervene effectively in the economy and increasingly called into question the feasibility of the state-centred accumulation model.

POSTSCRIPT

The policy changes of the mid-1980s constituted the initial phase of a reform process which intensified in 1988, when the Sandinista government introduced more sweeping economic stabilisation and adjustment measures. These were to have a dramatic effect on levels of living, particularly in urban areas where per capita consumption of basic foods fell by approximately 30 per cent between 1985 and 1989, and un- or under-employment increased markedly [*Utting, 1991*].

The pro-peasant orientation of some of the reform measures described above provided large sectors of the rural population with some protection from the shock treatment of the late 1980s. Such attempts to favour rural producers did little, however, to ensure support for the Sandinista regime. In February 1990, 64 per cent of rural voters joined 56 per cent of the urban electorate to oust the Sandinistas from government.

The 1990 elections brought a group to power which was intent on pursuing further reform, including the privatisation of state enterprises, drastic reduction in public expenditure and much tighter controls on credit, as well as greater deregulation of the grain market. These policies rapidly stabilised prices and the exchange rate, and to some extent benefited agro-export interests associated with coffee, beef and banana production, as well as with certain 'non-traditional' crops. But the levels of living of low-income urban and rural groups plummeted. The set of measures cushioning the fall of peasant and co-operative producers was abruptly eliminated, inducing a sharp decline in food production and reduction of grain prices.

In response to the resurgence of armed struggle in rural areas and protest actions taken by the main trade union organisations, and within a context of negotiations involving key sectors of Nicaraguan society, the present government has attempted to rethink some of its original policies. Agrarian reform has remained on the policy agenda and a significant minority share of reprivatised state assets has been allocated to workers. Meanwhile, for this government as for the previous one, the urban informal sector constitutes an uncertain political force: the number of people within it has grown rapidly and their level of living has been harshly affected by the general depression in the economy. Freedom to trade is hardly a panacea within this context, nor does it ensure political loyalty. Despite occasional fine tuning, the general orientation of government policy now favours the agro-export and large producer sectors of the economy.

REFERENCES

Argüello, A., Croes, E. and N. Kleiterp, 1987, *Nicaragua: Accumulación y transformación 1979–1985*, Managua: UNDP.
Avendaño, N., 1988, 'Caracterización general de las poíticas económicas en Nicaragua en el período 1980–1987', in CIERA (ed.), *El debate sobre la reforma ecónomica*, Managua: CIERA.
Barraclough, S. and P. Utting, 1986, 'Transition and Development in Nicaragua: Promise, Reality and Prospects', paper prepared for forthcoming UNU publication.

Barraclough, S., van Buren, A., Gariazzo, A., Sundaram, A. and P. Utting, 1988, *Aid That Counts: The Western Contribution to Development and Survival in Nicaragua*, Amsterdam: Transnational Institute.

Baumeister, E., 1988a, 'Comentarios', in CIERA (ed.), *El debate sobre la reforma ecónomica*, Managua: CIERA.

Baumeister, E., 1988b, 'Tres condicionantes político-ideológicos en la formulación de las políticas agrarias en Nicaragua', *Boletín Socio-Económico*, No. 7, Managua: INIES.

Bernales Alvarado, M., 1985, 'La transformación del estado: Problemas y perspectivas', in R. Harris and C. Vilas (eds.), *La revolución en Nicaragua*, Mexico City: Ediciones Era.

Biondi-Morra, B., 1988, 'Managing Food Policy Implementation in Developing Countries: The Case of the Nicaraguan State-Owned Agribusiness Enterprises 1979–1985', Doctoral Thesis, Harvard University.

Cabrales, R., 1987, 'El abastecimiento en ocho años de revolución', *Revista Nicaraguense de Ciencias Sociales*, Vol. 2, No. 3, pp. 41–47.

CIERA, 1984a, *El ABC del abastecimiento*, Managua: CIERA archive, Vol. 60.

CIERA, 1984b, *Participatory Democracy in Nicaragua*, Managua: CIERA.

CIERA, 1985, *Estudio de las cooperativas de producción*, CIERA archive, Vol. 72.

CIERA, 1986, *Alimentos, desarrollo y transición*, draft document prepared for the UNRISD Food Systems and Society Programme.

CIERA, 1987, *La problemàtica de la comercialización en Nicaragua*, CIERA archive, Vol. 82.

CIERA, 1989a, *La reforma agraria en Nicaragua, 1979–1989: El sistema alimentario*, Vol. II, Managua: CIERA.

CIERA, 1989b, *La reforma agraria en Nicaragua, 1979–1989: Organización y participación popular en el campo*, Vol. VI, Managua: CIERA.

CIERA and DGRA, 1987, *Balance de la poítica de acopio, precios y libre comercio de maíz y frijol: Primera y postrera, 1986/87*, CIERA archive, Vol. 78.

Delgado, R., 1986, 'Nicaragua: Los costos económicos de la agresión del gobierno de los Estados Unidos de Norte America', paper presented at V Nicaraguan Social Sciences Congress, Managua, 9–12 October 1986.

Dirección General de Fomento Campesino y Desarrollo Cooperativo (DGFCDC), 1988a, 'Situación actual del abastecimiento campesino', mimeo.

DGFCDC, 1988b, 'La red de distribución en el campo: Regiones I, V, VI', mimeo.

DGFCDC, 1988c, *Programa Nacional de Fomento a la Producción de Granos Básicos*, mimeo.

Dore, E., 1988, 'Nicaraguan Agrarian and Commercial Policy 1979–1988: Its Effect on the Peasantry', paper presented at a Symposium on the Nicaraguan Agrarian Reform, Amsterdam, Netherlands, 4–8 July 1988.

Enríquez, L., 1985, 'Social Transformation in Latin America: Tensions between Agro-Export Production and Agrarian Reform in Revolutionary Nicaragua', Ph.D. dissertation, University of California, Santa Cruz.

FitzGerald, E.V.K., 1985, 'La economía nacional en 1985', paper presented at IV Nicaraguan Social Sciences Congress, Managua, Aug.

FitzGerald, E.V.K., 1986, 'Notes on the Analysis of the Small Underdeveloped Economy in Transition', in R. Fagen *et al.* (eds.), *Transition and Development: Problems of Third World Socialism*, New York: Monthly Review Press/Center for the Study of the Americas.

FitzGerald, E.V.K., 1987, 'An Evaluation of the Economic Costs to Nicaragua of U.S. Aggression', in R. Spalding (ed.), *The Political Economy of Revolutionary Nicaragua*, Boston, MA: Allen & Unwin.

FitzGerald, E.V.K., 1988a, 'State Accumulation and Market Equilibria: An Application of Kalecki-Kornai Analysis to Planned Economies in the Third World', mimeo.

FitzGerald, E.V.K., 1988b, 'Problems in Financing a Revolution: Accumulation, Defence and Income Distribution in Nicaragua 1979–86', in E.V.K. FitzGerald and R. Vos (eds.), *Financing Economic Development: A Structuralist Approach to Monetary Policy*, London: Gower.

FitzGerald, E.V.K., 1989, 'Economic Crisis and Transition on the Periphery: The Case of Nicaragua', paper presented at UNRISD/ISER seminar on Economic Crisis and Third World Countries, Jamaica, 3–6 April 1989.

Flores-Estrada, M. and J. Lobo, 1986, 'La consigna es sobrevivir', *Pensamiento Propio*, No. 33, pp. 25–9.

IFAD, 1980, *Informe de la Misión Especial de Programación a Nicaragua*, Rome.

Instituto Histórico Centroamericano (IHCA), 1989, 'La organización campesina', *Envío*, No. 93, pp. 30–43.

Kaimowitz, D., 1986, 'Nicaraguan Debates on Agrarian Structure and Their Implications for Agricultural Policy and the Rural Poor', *Journal of Peasant Studies*, Vol. 14, No. 1.

Kleiterp, N., 1988, *Implementing a New Model of Accumulation: The Case of Nicaragua*, Working Paper No. 22, Sub-series on Money, Finance and Development, Institute of Social Studies, The Hague.

Luciak, I, 1987, 'Popular Democracy in the New Nicaragua: The Case of a Rural Mass Organization', *Comparative Politics*, Vol. 20, No. 1.

Marchetti, P. and C. Jerez, 1988, 'Democracy and Militarisation: War and Development', *IDS Bulletin*, Vol. 19, No. 3, pp. 1–11.

MICOIN, 1987, *Evaluación de las poíticas de abastecimiento nacional de 1986*, Managua: MICOIN.

Ministerio de Desarrollo Agropecuario y Reforma Agraria (MIDINRA), 1984, 'Problemas y perspectivas de la migración campo-ciudad', *Revolución y Desarrollo*, No. 3, pp. 19–23.

Núñez, D., 1989, 'A ocho años: La Unión Nacional de Agricultores y Ganaderos', *Cuadernos de Sociología* (Managua), No. 9–10, pp. 95–105.

Núñez, O., 1987, *Transición y lucha de clases en Nicaragua 1979–1986*, Mexico: CRIES/Siglo XXI.

Ortega, D., 1986, *Líneas del Plan Técnico Económico 1986*, Managua: Dirección de Información y Prensa de la Presidencia de la República de Nicaragua.

Pizarro, R., 1987, 'The New Economic Policy: A Necessary Readjustment', in R. Spalding (ed.), *The Political Economy of Revolutionary Nicaragua*, Boston, MA: Allen and Unwin.

Serra, L., 1988, 'Un proyecto impulsado desde la base', *Pensamiento Propio*, No. 52, pp. 32–5.

Stahler-Sholk, R., 1986, *La Normación del Trabajo en Nicaragua 1983–1986*, paper presented at V Nicaraguan Social Sciences Congress, Managua, 9–12 Oct. 1986.

Torres, R.M. and J.L. Coraggio, 1987, *Transición y crisis en Nicaragua*, San José: ICADIS.

Utting, P., 1983, 'La participación popular en el abastecimiento urbano: El caso de Managua', mimeo.

Utting, P., 1985, 'Limits to Change in a Post-Revolutionary Society: The Rise and Fall of Cheap Food Policy', mimeo.

Utting, P., 1987, 'Domestic Supply and Food Shortages', in R. Spalding (ed.), *The Political Economy of Revolutionary Nicaragua*, Boston, MA: Allen & Unwin.

Utting, P., 1988, *The Peasant Question and Development in Nicaragua*, UNRISD Discussion Paper No. 2, Geneva: UNRISD.

Utting, P., 1989, 'The Political Economy of Economic and Food Policy Reform in Third World Socialist Countries', Doctoral thesis, University of Essex.

Utting, P., 1991, *Economic Adjustment under the Sandinistas: Policy Reform, Food Security and Livelihood in Nicaragua*, Geneva: UNRISD.

Vilas, C., 1986a, 'El impacto de la transición revolucionaria en las clases populares: La clase obrera en la revolución sandinista', paper presented at V Nicaraguan Social Sciences Congress, Managua, 9–12 Oct. 1986.

Vilas, C., 1986b, 'The Mass Organizations in Nicaragua: The Current Problematic and Perspectives for the Future', *Monthly Review*, Nov.

Weeks, J., 1988, 'Private Entrepreneurship in a Revolutionary Context: A Case Study', Mimeo, Middlebury College, Vermont.

Wheelock, J., 1986, 'Balance y perspectivas de las poíticas de la revolución en el campo', in DAP/FSLN (ed.), *Líneas para el fortalecimiento de la alianza con el campesinado*, Managua: DAP/FSLN.

Wilson, P., 1987, 'Regionalization and Decentralization in Nicaragua', *Latin American Perspectives*, Vol. 14, No. 2, pp. 237–54.

Zalkin, M., 1985, 'Peasant Response to State Intervention in the Production of Basic Grains in Nicaragua: 1979–1984', Ph.D. dissertation, University of Massachusetts, Amherst.

Zalin, M., 1987, 'Food Policy and Class Transformation in Revolutionary Nicaragua, 1979–1986', *World Development*, Vol. 15, No. 7.

Zalkin, M., 1988, *Estructura de clases y el campesinado Nicaraguense: 1980, una nueva interpretación*, Managua: CIERA.